PROJECT MANAGEMENT
ADVENTURES
A Kid's Guide to Success

Dr. Joy Chacko

Skillful Adventures™ Series
www.SkillfulAdventures.com

Project Management Adventures: A Kid's Guide to Success

Originally published in 2025 by **Joy Chacko, PhD**

Part of the **Skillful Adventures™ Series**

ISBN: 979-8-9934027-3-4

(Economy Edition – Black & White Interior)

Publisher: Skillful Adventures Press

SkillfulAdventures.com

Featuring Engaging Project Adventures, Teamwork Challenges, and Simple Tools to Help Kids Plan, Lead, and Succeed!

These stories and activities complement the project management concepts and principles woven into a delightful narrative guided by The Friends and The Professor—helping children learn how to turn ideas into projects, and projects into success!

❇ Skillful Adventures™ Series ❇

✓ **Time Management Adventures** — Master time with fun strategies and daily success habits.

✓ **Project Management Adventures** — Turn ideas into projects and projects into success!

✓ **Mini-CFO Adventures** — Discover how money works and how to grow it wisely.

✓ **Leadership Adventures** — Build confidence, teamwork, and a vision that inspires.

And more Skillful Adventures™ are on the way!

❇ Visit **SkillfulAdventures.com**

Table of Contents

Section 1:

Building the Foundation

Discover what makes every great project succeed by learning the core steps, ideas, and teamwork foundations that set the stage for success.

Chapter 1

Introduction:
The Great Forest Festival

In a magical forest, where sunlight danced through the towering trees and sparkling streams whispered secrets of nature, a group of friends decided to do something truly spectacular. They wanted to organize the first-ever **Great Forest Festival**, a grand celebration of their woodland home.

Timmy the Tortoise, Bella the Bunny, Max the Monkey, and Lily the Ladybug were brimming with excitement.

"I'll gather flowers for the decorations!" said Bella, hopping with energy.

"I'll juggle bananas for the performance!" grinned Max, swinging from a branch.

"I'll make sure the festival banner looks perfect," offered Lily, unfurling her checklist.

"And I'll carry supplies to wherever they're needed," added Timmy with a calm nod.

Everyone had an idea, and they couldn't wait to get started.

The Project That Didn't Go As Planned

But as the festival day approached, chaos unfolded.

Bella was so busy hopping from one task to another that she forgot to finish the decorations.

Max was practicing his juggling but didn't teach the younger monkeys their part in the performance.

Timmy moved supplies slowly, but no one had told him where they needed to go.

Lily had too many tasks on her list and ran out of time to check on everyone's progress.

A week ahead of festival, they realized things weren't ready:

- Half the decorations were missing.
- The performers hadn't rehearsed.
- The food wasn't cooked.
- The banner was still rolled up.

The friends gathered at the **Sparkling Creek**, feeling frustrated and defeated.

"We worked so hard," sighed Bella. "Why did it turn out like this?"

Max scratched his head. "Maybe we just weren't meant to organize a festival."

Timmy shook his head slowly. "We tried our best, but something went wrong."

"I wish we knew how to do this properly," Lily murmured, looking at her half-finished checklist.

The Arrival of Professor ProjectManager

As the friends sat in silence, they heard a soft "hoot" from the trees. A wise voice broke the quiet.

"My friends, you didn't fail because you didn't try hard enough," the voice said kindly. "You failed because you didn't have a plan."

They looked up to see **Professor ProjectManager**, known fondly to the forest friends as **Professor Projecko**, the wisest owl in the forest. His golden eyes twinkled with wisdom, and his feathers ruffled gently as he adjusted his tiny spectacles.

"A plan?" asked Max, scratching his head.

"Yes," said the professor. "When we work on a big project, it's important to know where we're going, what we need, and how to get there. Without planning, even the best ideas can turn into a mess."

The friends leaned closer, their curiosity piqued.

"I can teach you the skills to turn your festival dreams into reality," the professor said. "Come to the **Golden Canopy**, and we'll begin with the most important step: **Planning**."

The friends exchanged hopeful glances. Maybe they could learn how to make the Great Forest Festival a success after all!

Meet the Heroes

Before we join the lesson, let's meet the team:

- **Timmy the Tortoise**: Calm and steady, Timmy always takes his time to think before he acts.

- **Bella the Bunny**: Quick and full of energy, Bella is always hopping from one activity to another, though sometimes too fast!

- **Max the Monkey**: Clever and curious, Max loves solving problems and finding fun ways to do things.

- **Lily the Ladybug**: Organized and thoughtful, Lily has a passion for making lists and helping her friends stay on track.

And, of course, there's the wise owl, **Professor Projecko**, who loves teaching others how to solve big problems step by step.

Reflection Time — What We Learned

As the moonlight shimmered over the forest, Professor Projecko gathered the friends beneath the Golden Canopy.

He asked softly:

- "How did it feel when things didn't go as planned?"

- "What made it hard to finish your tasks?"

- "What could a plan help us do next time?"

Bella's ears drooped. "I felt rushed and forgot some things."

Timmy nodded. "If we planned first, everyone would know what to do."

The professor smiled kindly. "Exactly. A good plan turns busy effort into teamwork—and helps every friend shine."

Key Takeaway for Kids

When friends take time to plan together—sharing ideas, roles, and steps—they save time later and enjoy building something wonderful side by side.

Final Inspiration

"Every dream grows stronger when it starts with a plan!"

Chapter 2

Planning – Define, Strategize, Organize, Execute

The friends gathered under the **Golden Canopy**, eager to hear what Professor Projecko had to say about turning their failed festival into a success.

"**Planning**," he began, unfurling a scroll on the ground, "is like creating a treasure map that helps you figure out:

1. **Where you're going.**
2. **What you need to get there.**
3. **The best way to reach your goal.**"

Timmy tilted his head thoughtfully. "So, planning means taking small steps instead of rushing ahead?"

"Exactly!" said the professor. "When you have a big project, planning helps you break it into smaller tasks so you don't feel overwhelmed. Let me explain why planning is so important."

Why Do We Plan?

The professor gestured to the remnants of their failed festival—a torn banner, unfinished decorations, and a pile of uneaten food.

"Do you remember what happened when you tried to organize the festival without a plan?" he asked.

Bella's ears drooped. "We forgot some tasks entirely, like decorating the stage."

"And I didn't finish juggling practice because no one reminded me," added Max, scratching his head.

"I spent so much time carrying supplies, but no one told me where to take them," said Timmy.

"And I had too many things on my list to manage," admitted Lily.

Professor ProjectManager nodded. "All these problems could have been avoided with a good plan. Planning helps us:

1. **Use resources wisely** – Like your time, materials, and energy.
2. **Stay organized** – So you know what to do next.

3. **Work as a team** – So everyone has a clear role and avoids stepping on each other's toes."

How Do We Plan?

Professor ProjectManager drew three big circles on his scroll. "Planning starts with three simple questions:

1. **What is the goal?** – What are we trying to achieve?
2. **What tasks are needed?** – What steps will help us get there?
3. **Who will do each task?** – Who is responsible for each step?"

The friends leaned in closer. "Once you answer these questions," the professor continued, "you can list the tasks in order and figure out what resources you need."

Max raised his hand. "Can we plan the festival again?"

"Wonderful idea!" said the professor. "Let's begin by reimagining your festival."

Reorganizing the Great Forest Festival

Professor ProjectManager picked up a stick and drew a large tree on the ground, representing the festival. "Now, let's plan step by step. First, what is your **goal**?"

"To have the best festival our forest has ever seen!" said Bella, hopping excitedly.

"Good. Now, let's break it into **tasks**," said the professor. He wrote them down as the friends called them out:

- **Decorations:** Hang banners and flowers.
- **Food:** Prepare forest snacks and drinks.
- **Performances:** Plan juggling, singing, and dancing.
- **Games:** Organize activities like leaf races and log balancing.

"And who will do each task?" asked the professor.

- Bella will handle decorations.
- Lily will organize the food team.
- Max will oversee performances and practice.
- Timmy will set up the games.

The professor added, "Remember, you'll all help each other when needed, but having leaders for each task keeps things organized."

Why This Plan Works

Professor ProjectManager tapped the scroll with his wing. "Do you see why this plan is better?"

Timmy nodded. "Because now we know who's doing what!"

"And we won't forget anything," added Bella.

"Exactly!" said the professor. "A good plan saves time, keeps you organized, and ensures everyone works together efficiently."

Rekindling Hope

With their tasks divided and roles assigned, the friends felt a surge of excitement.

"Do you think we can do it this time?" Lily asked.

"I know you can," said the professor. "You're already on your way to being excellent project managers."

Reflection Time — What We Learned

As the sun dipped behind the Golden Canopy, Professor Projecko asked:

- "How did planning make things clearer this time?"
- "What changed when everyone had a task to lead?"
- "Why does breaking a big goal into smaller steps help?"

Bella smiled. "It felt easier when we knew exactly what to do."

Timmy added, "And it was more fun working as a team."

The professor nodded proudly. "That's the power of a good plan—it turns confusion into confidence."

Key Takeaway for Kids

Planning helps you see the big picture, stay organized, and make teamwork smoother and more fun.

Final Inspiration

"Great planners turn big dreams into easy steps that lead to success!"

Chapter 3

Scope & Definition of Done

The forest friends gathered around a wide oak stump. Perched above them, Professor ProjectManager the wise owl spread out a colorful map of the Great Forest Festival grounds.

"Today," said the professor, fluffing his feathers, "we learn about **scope**. Scope means deciding what's *inside* our project—and what's *outside*. If it's on our festival map, it's included. If it's not, we say *'no' or 'not yet'*. That way, we can stay focused and finish strong."

Magic Map

The friends leaned in with eager eyes. Painted on the map were the stage, game stalls, snack corner, and a winding decorations path.

Timmy slowly traced his finger along the map. "So only these areas are our job?"

"Exactly!" said the professor. "Sticking to the map keeps us on track and helps us finish everything."

Bella's ears twitched. "But… what if I want balloons? And streamers? And maybe *lots* more flowers?"

The professor chuckled. "Ah, Bella, beware the **Scope Creep Monster**! Extra tasks sneak up and steal your time and energy."

The friends giggled as the professor sketched a silly monster with sticky hands reaching for balloons. (*From then on, the Scope Creep Monster became their funny reminder whenever new ideas popped up.*)

Goal Flags

Next, the professor handed each friend three bright paper flags.

"These are your **milestones**—mini goals that show you're on the right path," he explained.

- **Start Flag:** "Gather supplies"
- **Middle Flag:** "Set up stalls"
- **Finish Flag:** "Festival ready!"

The friends placed their flags on the map and cheered, knowing each step brought them closer to success.

Done Checklist

Max flipped open a giant leaf notebook. "Let's make a **Done Checklist**!" he declared.

Together, they wrote:

- Banner hung
- Stage ready
- Games set
- Snacks chilled

"Whenever we finish one," Max said proudly, "we tick the box—and celebrate! A cheer, a little dance, or even a silly bunny hop!"

Bella happily ticked the first box, and the whole group burst into a hopping dance.

Milestone Moments

At the **start flag**, Timmy carefully drew a tiny turtle shell to mark the moment.

At the **middle flag**, Lily wrote in her journal: "Setting up stalls was fun because everyone helped."

At the **finish flag**, the professor snapped a smiling group photo.

Scope Creep Monster Returns

Suddenly, Bella bounced up again. "What if we add a Ferris wheel? Or three more snack stands?"

The professor raised the doodled monster. "Remember: too many extras make the Scope Creep Monster stronger. Always ask: *Is this on the map?* If not, save it for another time."

Bella laughed. "Okay, Monster—you'll have to wait for the next festival!"

Reflection Time — What We Learned

As the stars twinkled above the forest, Professor Projecko gathered the friends by the glowing map.

He asked quietly:

- "What helped us stay focused on our plan today?"
- "How did knowing what's inside our project make work easier?"
- "When should we say 'not yet' to new ideas?"

Bella giggled. "We stopped the Scope Creep Monster before he could grab our time!"

Timmy nodded. "And we finished what we started!"

The professor smiled. "That's true wisdom—knowing what belongs now and what can wait."

Key Takeaway for Kids

Stay focused on what's inside your project. When you finish what you start, success—and celebration—will follow.

Final Inspiration

"Smart project managers know when to say yes—and when to save ideas for later!"

Chapter 4

Dependency Management –
Working Together, Step by Step

The friends had made great progress with their plan for the Great Forest Festival. Under Professor ProjectManager's guidance, they had written down their goal, identified the tasks, and even assigned some roles. Now, Bella the Bunny, Max the Monkey, Timmy the Tortoise, and Lily the Ladybug were ready to get started.

Or so they thought.

Eager to Begin

Bella hopped excitedly around the clearing. "I'll start hanging the banners now!" she announced.

Professor ProjectManager raised a feathered eyebrow. "Hold on, Bella. Are the banners ready yet?"

Bella froze mid-hop. "Well... no. But I can still start hanging them, right?"

"Not quite," said the professor, adjusting his tiny spectacles. "You see, Bella, there's something important we need to figure out before you dive in. It's called **Dependency Management**."

What Is Dependency Management?

The friends gathered around the professor as he spread out a scroll on the ground. It showed a web of tasks connected by arrows.

"Dependency Management," began Professor ProjectManager, "is about understanding how tasks relate to one another. Some tasks depend on others being completed first, while others can happen at the same time. Figuring out these relationships is like building a bridge—you can't put up the middle part until the supports on each end are ready."

Timmy tilted his head. "So, some things have to be done in a certain order?"

"Exactly!" said the professor. "When we identify task dependencies, we discover:

1. **What needs to be done first** – Tasks that must be completed before others can start.

2. **What can happen at the same time** – Tasks that can be done in parallel to save time."

The Festival Tasks

The professor turned to the group. "Let's take another look at your festival tasks. Which ones do you think depend on others?"

Lily buzzed thoughtfully. "The food preparation depends on gathering ingredients first."

Max nodded. "And my juggling act depends on having the stage ready."

Bella's ears twitched. "Oh, so… the banners can't be hung until the poles and ropes are set up!"

Professor ProjectManager smiled. "Exactly! Now you're starting to see the connections. By understanding dependencies, we can make sure no one gets stuck waiting for another task to be finished."

Parallel and Series Tasks

The professor used his claw to draw two lines on the scroll. One was straight, with arrows pointing in order:

Task A → Task B → Task C

"These are **series tasks**," he explained. "They must be done one after the other. For example, you can't cook food until you gather ingredients."

Then he drew two lines running side by side:

Task X → Task Y

Task Z → Task W

"These are **parallel tasks**," he continued. "They can happen at the same time. For example, while Timmy sets up the Leaf Race, Bella can decorate the stage."

The friends nodded, starting to see how their tasks fit together.

A Shift in Plans

Bella looked at the professor. "So... since the poles and ropes aren't ready yet, I can't hang the banners right now."

"That's right," said the professor. "But there's no need to sit idle. Let's find another task you can work on in parallel."

Bella thought for a moment. "I could start preparing the flower garlands for the stage!"

"Perfect!" said the professor. "That way, you're still making progress while we wait for the poles and ropes to be set up."

Why Dependency Management Matters

Professor ProjectManager gathered the group around. "When you manage dependencies well, you:

1. **Avoid delays** – No one is waiting around for something to get done.
2. **Save time** – Parallel tasks help you finish the project faster.
3. **Work efficiently** – Everyone knows what they can do and when."

Timmy nodded slowly. "It's like building a sandcastle. You can dig the moat and build the walls at the same time, but you can't fill the moat with water until the digging is done."

"Exactly!" said the professor. "Dependency Management helps you keep things flowing smoothly."

The Team in Action

With their tasks reorganized, the friends got to work. Max practiced juggling while Timmy set up the Leaf Race logs. Bella busily wove flower garlands, ready to hang them once the poles were up. Lily buzzed between the food team and the stage crew, helping wherever she was needed.

By understanding their task dependencies, the team stayed productive and avoided getting stuck.

The Festival Begins to Shine

By the end of the day, the friends looked around and smiled. The festival was starting to come together beautifully.

Bella hopped happily. "I'm so glad I didn't waste time waiting to hang the banners."

"And I'm glad we worked on things in the right order," added Timmy.

Professor ProjectManager's golden eyes twinkled with pride. "Great work, everyone. You're learning how to work smarter, not harder. With Dependency Management, you're building a festival—and teamwork—that everyone will remember."

Reflection Time — What We Learned

As the evening breeze rustled the trees, Professor Projecko asked:

- "What did we learn about the order of our tasks today?"
- "How did working in the right sequence help everyone stay busy?"
- "Why is it smart to plan which tasks depend on others?"

Bella smiled. "I didn't have to wait around—I found something useful to do!"

Timmy nodded. "And we finished faster because everyone kept moving."

The professor beamed. "That's the heart of teamwork—knowing when to wait, when to help, and when to move ahead."

Key Takeaway for Kids

When you know which tasks depend on others, you can work smarter, stay productive, and help your team finish faster.

Final Inspiration

"Step by step, great teams keep moving—because every task connects to the next!"

Chapter 5

The Critical Path – Finding the Most Important Steps

Under the shade of the **Golden Canopy**, the friends were busy working on tasks for the Great Forest Festival. Timmy the Tortoise was carefully setting up the logs for the Leaf Race, Bella the Bunny was arranging flower garlands for the stage, and Max the Monkey was juggling coconuts for his big performance.

Nearby, Lily the Ladybug was putting the finishing touches on the festival's honey and berry refreshments. She took a step back to admire her work and smiled. "Done!" she said, brushing off her tiny hands.

As Lily buzzed around to check on her friends, two voices called out at the same time.

"Lily, can you help me?" Bella shouted. "I can't reach the high branches to hang the banner!"

"Lily, over here!" Timmy called out. "I need help moving these logs—they're too heavy for me alone."

Lily froze in midair, unsure of what to do. "Oh no," she said. "Who should I help first?"

Professor ProjectManager, perched on a low branch nearby, saw the commotion and flapped his wings. "Ah, what a perfect moment to talk about the **Critical Path**!"

What Is the Critical Path?

The professor adjusted his tiny glasses and spread a new scroll on the ground. It showed a web of tasks, all connected by arrows pointing toward a big sun labeled "Festival Day."

"Lily, before you decide whom to help, let's figure out which task is on the **Critical Path**," he said.

Bella twitched her ears. "What's the Critical Path?"

Professor ProjectManager smiled. "The Critical Path is the sequence of tasks that must be completed on time for the project to succeed. If a task on the critical path is delayed, the entire project is delayed."

Timmy nodded slowly. "So, some tasks are more urgent than others?"

"Exactly!" said the professor. "Not every task needs to be done immediately. Some have extra time, called 'slack,' while others have no slack at all. Tasks with no slack are on the critical path, and those must be completed first."

Choosing Who to Help

Professor ProjectManager turned to Bella. "Let's start with your task. What happens if the banner isn't hung on time?"

Bella thought for a moment. "The stage might look plain, but the games and performances can still happen, right?"

"Good observation," said the professor. "Now, Timmy, what happens if the logs for the Leaf Race aren't ready on time?"

Timmy looked worried. "The Leaf Race will be delayed, and if the games don't start on time, it'll throw off the whole schedule."

Professor ProjectManager nodded. "Exactly. The Leaf Race is on the critical path because its delay would affect the entire festival. The banner, while important, has some slack—it can be finished a bit later without impacting the schedule."

Lily buzzed thoughtfully. "So, I should help Timmy first?"

"That's right!" said the professor. "Focusing on the critical path ensures the festival stays on track. Once Timmy's task is finished, you can help Bella with her banner."

The Critical Path Method (CPM)

The professor tapped the scroll with his wing. "This is called the **Critical Path Method**, or CPM. It's a way to identify the tasks that are most important for keeping a project on schedule. CPM helps project managers:

1. **Identify the critical path** – The tasks that must be completed on time.

2. **Manage resources wisely** – By focusing help where it's needed most.

3. **Avoid delays** – By solving problems on the critical path first."

Max swung down from a branch, juggling coconuts. "It's like finding the fastest way to finish a puzzle. You start with the pieces that connect everything else!"

Professor ProjectManager chuckled. "Exactly, Max. The critical path is like the backbone of a project—support it first, and everything else will fall into place."

Applying the Lesson

With their new understanding, Lily flew to help Timmy. Together, they moved the logs into place, ensuring the Leaf Race could start on time. Once the logs were set, Lily and Timmy both pitched in to help Bella hang the banner, completing it just in time for the festival's opening ceremony.

"You see," said the professor, "by helping the critical path first, you avoided delays and kept the festival running smoothly. That's the power of prioritizing tasks wisely."

Keeping the Festival on Track

As the festival day approached, the friends applied the Critical Path Method to every part of their work. They double-checked the critical tasks and supported one another when it mattered most.

Bella smiled as she admired the completed stage. "This festival is going to be amazing."

"And all because we stayed focused on the most important steps," Timmy added, his voice steady with pride.

Professor ProjectManager's golden eyes twinkled. "With your teamwork and understanding of the critical path, I have no doubt this will be a festival to remember."

Reflection Time — What We Learned

As the lanterns glowed softly in the forest, Professor Projecko asked:

- "How did knowing the most important steps help us stay on schedule?"
- "What happens if a task on the critical path is delayed?"
- "Why is it smart to help with the most urgent work first?"

Lily smiled. "Helping Timmy first kept everything on time!"

Bella nodded. "And we still finished the banner later—without rushing."

The professor's eyes gleamed. "That's how great planners think—focus first where it matters most."

Key Takeaway for Kids

Every big goal has a few tasks that matter most. When you finish those first, the whole project stays strong and on track.

Final Inspiration

"Focus on what matters most—because the critical steps lead the way to success!"

Chapter 6

Prioritization – Effective Utilization of Time & Resources

The Great Forest Festival was just days away, and the friends were working harder than ever to get everything ready. Timmy the Tortoise was double-checking the Leaf Race setup, Max the Monkey was perfecting his juggling routine, and Lily the Ladybug was coordinating the food team.

Bella the Bunny, meanwhile, was entirely absorbed in her task: creating the most beautiful floral decorations the forest had ever seen. She hopped from flower to flower, weaving intricate garlands, tying bows, and arranging colorful blossoms into elaborate shapes.

But as the day went on, Professor ProjectManager noticed something. While Bella's decorations were stunning, she hadn't finished decorating the stage or the festival entrance.

"Bella," the professor called gently, flapping down to her workstation. "How are the decorations coming along?"

Bella twitched her ears proudly. "Just look at this bouquet, Professor! It's a masterpiece!"

"It is beautiful," the professor agreed, examining the arrangement. "But let me ask you—how many of the festival guests will see this bouquet compared to the stage and the entrance?"

Bella paused. "Well… the stage and the entrance will be seen by everyone, but this bouquet will only go on the refreshment table."

"Ah," said the professor, his golden eyes twinkling. "Then perhaps it's time to talk about **Prioritization** and something called the **80/20 Rule**."

What Is Prioritization?

The friends gathered around as Professor ProjectManager unfurled a scroll.

"Prioritization," he began, "is about focusing on the most important tasks first, especially when time or resources are limited. It ensures you spend your energy where it matters most."

He drew a quick chart on the scroll, showing a line that read:

Time & Resources → Tasks → Impact on Success

"By prioritizing, you make sure the tasks with the biggest impact on your project are completed first," he explained.

Timmy nodded slowly. "So, it's like eating the biggest leaves first so you don't run out of energy?"

"Exactly, Timmy!" said the professor.

The 80/20 Rule

Professor ProjectManager tapped his chart with his claw. "There's a principle called the **80/20 Rule**, also known as the **Pareto Principle**. It says that 20% of your tasks can produce 80% of your results. By identifying that 20%, you can focus on the work that really makes a difference."

Max's eyes lit up. "So... if we do the most important 20%, we get most of the results without doing everything?"

"Precisely!" said the professor. "For example, in your floral decorations, Bella, 20% of the work—like decorating the stage and the entrance—will create 80% of the impact. These are the areas every guest will see. Once those are done, you can spend time on the finer details, like bouquets and table arrangements."

Bella's ears drooped. "Oh no! I've been spending all my time on the bouquets!"

"That's not a mistake," the professor reassured her. "Your work is beautiful, but it's important to prioritize the decorations that will make the biggest difference first."

Applying Prioritization

Bella hopped to the center of the clearing. "Okay, I'll start with the stage and the entrance right away!"

"Great idea," said Lily. "And while you do that, I'll gather more flowers for you so you can focus on decorating."

Max grinned. "And I'll move the bouquet to the refreshment table—it looks great there!"

Timmy chimed in. "See? Prioritizing doesn't mean your other work isn't important. It just means getting the biggest things done first."

Bella smiled. "Thanks, everyone! I'll make the stage and entrance decorations as beautiful as possible."

Why Prioritization Matters

As Bella worked on the stage and entrance, Professor ProjectManager gathered the group again.

"Prioritization helps you:

1. **Use time and resources wisely** – You focus on what matters most.

2. **Avoid last-minute stress** – The big tasks are done early, so there's time for finishing touches.

3. **Maximize impact** – You ensure the most important parts of your project are completed on time."

Max swung down from a tree, juggling his coconuts. "It's like juggling! If I start with the heaviest coconuts, I can balance the lighter ones later!"

The professor chuckled. "Exactly, Max. Prioritization helps you balance your time and energy."

The Festival Comes Together

By the end of the day, Bella had completed the stage and entrance decorations. As the sun set over the magical forest, the friends stood together, admiring their progress.

"The stage looks amazing!" Bella said, her voice filled with pride.

"And the entrance is so welcoming," Lily added.

Professor ProjectManager's golden eyes twinkled. "You see? By prioritizing, you made sure the most important tasks were finished first. That's the key to effective time and resource management."

Timmy nodded. "One step at a time—and the biggest steps first!"

Reflection Time — What We Learned

As the sun dipped low, Professor Projecko asked with a gentle smile:

- "How did focusing on the biggest tasks first help today?"

- "What happens when we spend too much time on smaller details?"

- "How can we use the 80/20 rule in our own projects?"

Bella laughed softly. "When I started with the stage and entrance, everything came together faster!"

Timmy nodded. "And it looked amazing without rushing at the end."

The professor twinkled. "That's the power of prioritizing—put your best time where it matters most."

Key Takeaway for Kids

When you start with the most important tasks, you save time, reduce stress, and make a bigger difference with your work.

Final Inspiration

"Do first what matters most—and the rest will shine even brighter!"

Section 2:

Teamwork, Communication & Systems Thinking

Discover how to make projects succeed by sharing jobs with pride, inviting others to help, spotting how things connect (systems thinking), and running quick daily check-ins so everyone stays included and the team can shine.

Chapter 7

Roles, Communication
& Daily Check-ins

The morning sun glowed through the forest as the festival team gathered around their oak stump. Professor ProjectManager spread out a new set of brightly colored cards.

"Every successful project needs clear **roles** and good **communication**," he explained. "When everyone knows their job and checks in often, the team stays strong."

Team Badges

The professor lifted each card one by one.

- **The Organizer** keeps track of everything that needs doing, so nothing gets forgotten. Timmy became the Organizer, steady and thoughtful, who loves making sure nothing is forgotten.

- **The Helper** jumps in to help whenever it's needed because teamwork makes everything easier. Bella hopped proudly as the Helper, always ready to support her friends.

- **The Checker** double-checks tasks to make sure nothing is missed. Max grinned as the Checker, happy to spot little details others might miss.

- **The Reporter** shares updates with the whole group so everyone stays informed. Lily fluttered happily as the Reporter, excited to tell stories and keep everyone connected.

"Now decorate your badges," said the professor. "Use your favorite colors, shapes, or drawings to make them special. When you decorate your own badge, you feel proud and remember your job better. Decorating your badge builds role ownership and identity—it reminds you why your role matters to the whole team."

The friends drew stars, flowers, and smiley faces on their badges, then pinned them proudly to their chests.

Stand-Up Huddle

"Now we practice our **daily huddle**," the professor said.

He reminded them: "While someone is talking, listen carefully and don't interrupt. Listening quietly shows you respect your friends and helps the team work well."

Then he paused, looking each friend in the eye.

"Listen. Listen. Listen… listen! In project management, listening is critical. If you don't listen to your friends—or to your clients and their needs—a project can fall miserably. Some even say if you spend 90% of your time listening, only 10% is needed to find the solution."

The group nodded thoughtfully, then chanted their motto loudly together:

"One voice at a time, we listen and shine!"

Each friend shared in turn:

- "Yesterday I…" (what they did)

- "Today I…" (what they will do)

- "I'm stuck on…" (any problem)

- "I need help with…" (ask for support)

The huddle was a quick check-in that kept everyone focused and energized.

Active Listening Game

"Let's practice listening with extra focus," said the professor.

Timmy spoke, and Bella repeated what she heard. Max and Lily nodded, keeping their eyes on him.

The professor reminded them with a chant:

"Look with your eyes, nod your head, keep your mouth quiet until it's your turn."

He added: "Repeat in your own words what your friend said—that shows you understand."

Then he smiled: "If you forget to listen, do a silly dance to remind us all to listen carefully."

Everyone laughed as Max wiggled through a monkey dance. Soon, the group was practicing *super-listening* with smiles.

Show-and-Tell Posters

Lily suggested: "Let's make little **posters** to show progress!"

They used simple pictures and colors:

- Green = finished
- Yellow = halfway
- Red = needs work

"Keep symbols and colors simple," Lily said wisely, "but you can also add your own drawings or stickers to make the poster feel uniquely yours."

Feedback Stars

At the end of the meeting, the friends gave each other **Feedback Stars**: one positive and one suggestion.

"Max kept us on schedule," said Bella. "   Star for you!"

Timmy added gently, "Maybe we could check the snack table now and then to keep it tidy."

The professor reminded them: "Rotate who gives feedback each day. That way, everyone learns how to give and receive feedback fairly."

Inclusion Feature

"Did every voice get heard today?" asked the professor.

Lily raised her tiny wing. "Sometimes I feel quiet."

Bella offered, "Next time I'll ask, 'Would you like to share, Lily?'"

The professor nodded. "That's called a **shy-friend check**. And if you feel shy, it's okay! You can share in your own way—maybe with a picture, a thumbs-up, or just one word. Friends can also notice if someone looks quiet and invite them gently with a smile or kind word. Sometimes a smile or kind word helps everyone feel welcome. What matters is that every voice is included."

Reflection Time — What We Learned

As the forest quieted for the evening, Professor Projecko asked with a gentle smile:

- "How did clear roles help our teamwork today?"
- "Why is listening so important during check-ins?"
- "How can we make sure every voice is heard?"

Bella said, "When we listened, no one felt left out."

Lily added softly, "And everyone's ideas made our plan better."

The professor nodded proudly. "That's what true teamwork sounds like—many voices working as one."

Key Takeaway for Kids

When everyone knows their role, listens carefully, and checks in daily, the whole team stays connected, confident, and kind.

Final Inspiration

"Great teams listen, share, and shine—together every day!"

Chapter 8

Engaging Stakeholders – Input, Support, and Collaboration

The Great Forest Festival was shaping up wonderfully. The team had made excellent progress on their individual tasks, but Professor ProjectManager noticed something important: the rest of the forest community hadn't been involved yet.

"Friends," he said, landing gracefully near the group, "you've done a fantastic job so far. But a festival isn't just about the organizers—it's about everyone in the community. Have you thought about involving other forest residents?"

Max the Monkey swung down from a tree. "Involve them? Like how?"

"By engaging stakeholders," the professor explained.

What Are Stakeholders?

"Stakeholders are the people who are affected by or have an interest in your project," Professor ProjectManager began. "For our festival, stakeholders include everyone who will attend, contribute, or help in some way."

Lily the Ladybug buzzed thoughtfully. "So… the birds, squirrels, and bees are all stakeholders?"

"Exactly," the professor said. "Stakeholders can provide ideas, resources, and support that make your project even better. Engaging them early builds excitement and ensures the festival meets everyone's needs."

Engaging Stakeholders

The friends paused to think about how the festival could involve more of the community. Each one started brainstorming ideas:

- **Timmy the Tortoise** suggested a workshop on sustainable living, inviting the squirrels to teach how to build birdhouses from fallen branches.

- **Bella the Bunny** proposed a craft competition for the younger animals, with prizes for the most creative entries.

- **Max the Monkey** wanted to add live music performances and decided to ask the birds to form a choir.

- **Lily the Ladybug** thought of organizing food stalls where forest residents could sell treats made from berries, honey, and nuts.

"That's a wonderful start," said Professor ProjectManager, smiling. "Now comes the next step: reaching out to the stakeholders to gather their input and ensure their needs are considered."

Excited, the friends split up to connect with their chosen groups:

- **Timmy** spoke to the squirrels, who were thrilled to teach the sustainable living workshop.

- **Bella** announced the craft competition to the younger animals, who eagerly started gathering materials.

- **Max** swung into the trees to talk to the birds, who loved the idea of forming a choir.

- **Lily** buzzed through the meadow, rallying the bees and food stall owners to prepare delicious treats.

As they worked, the friends realized that engaging stakeholders wasn't just about asking for help—it was about building relationships and creating a shared vision for the festival.

How to Engage Stakeholders

The professor later gathered the group and explained the steps for effective stakeholder engagement:

1. **Identify Stakeholders**

   ◊   "Think about who will attend the festival, who will contribute, and who might be impacted by it."

2. **Ask for Input**

   ◊   "Stakeholders often have great ideas or concerns you might not have thought about. Asking for their input shows that you value their opinion."

3. **Collaborate for Support**

   ◊ "Stakeholders can help in ways you might not expect. For example, the bees could help with decorations made from wax, or the fireflies could help with festival lighting."

4. **Share the Vision**

   ◊ "Explain your festival's goals and how everyone's contributions will make it a success."

Introducing PERT

During a break, Max swung down from the trees and asked, "Professor, some of the stakeholders have different ideas about how long their tasks will take. How do we figure out the schedule?"

"That's a great question," said the professor. "In situations like this, we can use a tool called the **Program Evaluation Review Technique**, or **PERT**. It helps estimate how long a task might take by considering three scenarios:

1. The fastest time (**optimistic**) – If everything goes perfectly.

2. The slowest time (**pessimistic**) – If there are delays.

3. The most likely time – What usually happens based on experience."

"For example," the professor continued, "if the food stall team thinks it will take 2 hours in the best case, 6 hours in the worst case, and 4 hours realistically, PERT helps us find the expected time."

Lily buzzed thoughtfully. "How does it work?"

"It's simple," said the professor. "You can use this formula:

Expected Time = (Optimistic + 4 × Most Likely + Pessimistic) ÷ 6

Let's calculate:

- Optimistic (O) = 2 hours

- Most Likely (M) = 4 hours

- Pessimistic (P) = 6 hours

Expected Time (E) = (2 + 4 × 4 + 6) ÷ 6

E = (2 + 16 + 6) ÷ 6 = 24 ÷ 6 = **4 hours**

"So," said the professor, "the food stalls should take about 4 hours to set up."

Lily buzzed with excitement. "That's so helpful!"

"Exactly," said the professor. "PERT helps create realistic schedules by considering both the best- and worst-case scenarios while focusing on what's most likely to happen."

Why Engaging Stakeholders Matters

When the friends regrouped, Professor ProjectManager shared a real-world example:

"Imagine you're organizing a school event, like a science fair," he said. "Stakeholders might include teachers, students, and parents. Teachers could help with rules and judging, students could present projects, and parents might contribute materials or snacks. By engaging each group, you create a better event and make sure everyone feels included."

Bella's ears twitched. "So, by working with the squirrels, birds, and bees, we're making the festival better for everyone?"

"Exactly," said the professor. "Engaging stakeholders brings fresh ideas and ensures the project meets everyone's needs."

The Festival Takes Shape

Thanks to PERT and their collaboration with stakeholders, the team created a schedule that accounted for uncertainties, ensuring every part of the festival— food stalls, craft competitions, and performances—would be ready on time.

Timmy looked at the schedule and nodded slowly. "This makes everything feel less overwhelming."

"And it gives us time to enjoy the festival too!" added Bella with a bright smile.

Professor ProjectManager's eyes twinkled. "When you use tools like PERT and engage your stakeholders effectively, you're not just managing tasks—you're building a stronger community. That's the secret to a successful project!"

Reflection Time — What We Learned

As the forest glowed with evening light, Professor Projecko asked warmly:

- "How did involving others make the festival better?"
- "What did we learn from listening to our stakeholders' ideas?"
- "Why is teamwork stronger when more voices are included?"

Lily buzzed proudly. "The bees and birds made the festival more colorful and fun!"

Timmy nodded. "And everyone felt like part of the team."

The professor smiled. "That's the power of collaboration—when everyone belongs, the project truly shines."

Key Takeaway for Kids

When you include others, listen to their ideas, and work together, your project becomes richer, stronger, and more meaningful.

Final Inspiration

"Great leaders don't work alone—they build success together with every voice that cares!"

Chapter 9

Systems Thinking – Seeing the Big Picture

Everything was nearly set for the big celebration. Decorations adorned the trees, food stalls buzzed with activity, and workshops were set to teach everything from sustainable living to nature crafts. But just as everything seemed to be coming together, the friends hit a roadblock.

Max the Monkey swung into the clearing, looking frazzled. "The bird choir says they need more space to practice, but the food stalls are already taking up the clearing! How are we supposed to make this work?"

Timmy the Tortoise added, "And the craft competition is supposed to happen nearby. If we move the choir, it'll disturb the competition."

Bella the Bunny twitched her ears. "It feels like everything is connected, and one problem is causing another!"

Professor ProjectManager landed nearby, his golden eyes twinkling. "Ah, my friends, you've just stumbled upon the magic of **Systems Thinking**!"

What Is Systems Thinking?

Professor ProjectManager spread his wings and gestured at the festival site. "A project isn't just a collection of tasks. It's a system, where everything is interconnected. **Systems Thinking** means understanding how all the parts work together to create the whole. It's about seeing the big picture."

Lily the Ladybug buzzed thoughtfully. "So, it's not just about solving one problem—it's about seeing how fixing one thing might affect everything else?"

"Exactly," said the professor. "When you look at a project as a system, you start to see:

1. **Interconnections** – How different tasks and decisions are linked.
2. **Complexity** – How small changes can ripple through the entire system.
3. **The Big Picture** – How every part contributes to the success of the whole project."

The Web of Complexity

The professor drew a simple diagram on the ground:

- **Bird Choir Space → Food Stall Placement → Craft Competition Area → Workshop Schedule → Lighting Setup → Guest Traffic Flow**

"These are just a few of the interconnections," he explained. "Each part affects the others. Moving the bird choir to a new location might free up space, but it could also create noise near the workshops. That's why we need to think about how every change ripples through the whole system."

Lily buzzed thoughtfully. "It feels like everything in the festival is connected, more than we realize. We should think about all the remaining activities in a holistic manner—using Systems Thinking!"

Professor ProjectManager smiled. "Exactly, Lily. When you think holistically, you can see the interconnections and find solutions that work for the whole system, not just one part."

Max scratched his head. "So... how do we solve this without making things worse?"

"By looking at the big picture and asking the right questions," said the professor, gesturing at the diagram:

1. **What's the goal of the system?** – A smooth and enjoyable festival for everyone.

2. **What are the key parts of the system?** – Decorations, performances, food stalls, workshops, lighting, and guest flow.

3. **How do these parts affect one another?** – For example, moving the bird choir impacts both sound levels and available space.

Bella twitched her ears. "It's like a puzzle. If you move one piece, you have to make sure the others still fit together!"

Solving the Problem

The friends worked together to map out the interconnections:

- The **bird choir** needed a quiet, open space to practice.
- The **craft competition** required a nearby area for kids to concentrate.
- The **food stalls** had to stay central for easy access.

"Let's think about the big picture," said the professor. "What's the best way to balance everyone's needs?"

Timmy suggested moving the bird choir to a nearby grove, slightly farther from the main festival area but still accessible. Bella added that the craft competition could shift closer to the edge of the clearing, creating a quieter space. Lily suggested reorganizing the food stalls to free up more central space.

Max grinned. "And I can help the birds set up their new practice spot to make it extra special!"

With their plan in place, the friends realized they could solve the problem by thinking about the system as a whole rather than each part in isolation.

Why Systems Thinking Matters

After everything was reorganized, Professor ProjectManager gathered the team.

"Great work, everyone! By using Systems Thinking, you:

1. **Managed complexity** – You saw how all the parts were connected and worked to balance them.

2. **Avoided new problems** – You considered how changes to one part might affect others.

3. **Created harmony** – You ensured every part of the festival worked together as a whole."

Bella twitched her ears. "It's like weaving a tapestry. If one thread is out of place, the whole picture looks wrong."

"Exactly," said the professor. "And that's why Systems Thinking is so powerful—it helps you see and manage the big picture."

Real-Life Systems Thinking

The professor shared an example to make the concept even clearer:

"Imagine you're organizing a school play. If you focus only on the costumes, you might forget how they need to match the set design or lighting. Systems Thinking means considering how all the parts—costumes, sets, lights, and actors—work together to create a successful performance."

Timmy nodded slowly. "So, Systems Thinking helps us see how everything is connected, like the gears in a clock."

"Exactly," said the professor. "It's the key to managing complexity in any project."

The Festival Unites

As the festival day approached, the friends felt confident. They had organized the bird choir, the craft competition, the food stalls, and the workshops in a way that made everything flow smoothly.

On the big day, the bird choir's songs filled the air, the kids' crafts amazed everyone, and the food stalls buzzed with happy customers.

"This is the best festival ever," said Bella, hopping with excitement.

"And it's all because we looked at the big picture," added Lily.

Professor ProjectManager's eyes twinkled. "Great projects, like great festivals, succeed when every part works together. Systems Thinking helps you manage complexity and create something truly extraordinary."

Reflection Time — What We Learned

As the stars sparkled above, Professor Projecko gathered the friends beneath the glowing lanterns and asked:

- "What happened when we looked at how everything was connected?"
- "How did seeing the big picture help us solve the space problem?"
- "Why is it important to think about how one change affects everything else?"

Bella smiled. "When we looked at the whole festival, the pieces fit together perfectly."

Timmy nodded. "It felt good to fix one problem without causing another."

The professor beamed. "That's the wisdom of Systems Thinking—seeing how every part works together to make the whole shine."

Key Takeaway for Kids

When you look at the big picture and understand how things connect, you can solve problems more wisely and create harmony in every project.

Final Inspiration

"See the whole picture—because every small piece helps the system work beautifully!"

Chapter 10

Teamwork –
Everyone Has a Role

The festival grounds buzzed. Everything was nearly in place, and the magical forest was electric with excitement. Decorations were nearly complete, the bird choir rehearsals filled the air with music, and food stalls were buzzing with activity. Yet, as the festival day approached, the friends began to feel overwhelmed.

"I feel like there's too much to do!" Bella the Bunny exclaimed, hopping nervously. "What if something gets missed?"

Lily the Ladybug buzzed by, her lists fluttering in the breeze. "We have so many tasks left! How do we make sure everything gets done in time?"

Professor ProjectManager perched on a nearby branch, observing their stress. "Ah, my friends, this is the perfect moment to talk about Teamwork," he said. "Teamwork helps us share the load and make sure no one feels stuck."

What Is Teamwork?

Professor ProjectManager hopped down to the ground. "Teamwork means working together, where each member plays an important role based on their strengths. It's not just about dividing tasks; it's about supporting one another and making sure everyone feels valued."

Timmy the Tortoise raised his head. "But what if one person has too much to do and can't finish in time?"

"That's why you check in with each other," said the professor. "Helping the person who's stuck makes the whole team stronger."

The Roles of the Team

The professor turned to the friends. "Let's think about your strengths and how they can contribute to the festival. Each of you has a unique role to play."

- **Timmy the Tortoise:** Calm and steady — keeps the schedule and checks that tasks are on track.

- **Bella the Bunny:** Energetic and creative — leads decorations and boosts team energy.

- **Max the Monkey:** Clever and resourceful — solves problems and handles tricky fixes.
- **Lily the Ladybug:** Organized and thoughtful — keeps the checklist and signs everything up.

"See?" the professor said with a smile. "When you each play to your strengths, the whole team works like a well-oiled machine."

Solving a Team Problem

As they talked, Timmy noticed Max juggling coconuts nervously.

"Max, are you okay?" Timmy asked.

Max sighed. "I'm supposed to fix the bird choir's stage, but I also need to test the lights for the evening show. I don't think I can do both in time."

Lily buzzed over. "Let's all help! I can work on the lights while you focus on the stage."

"And I'll make sure the schedule adjusts so we're not rushed," added Timmy.

Bella hopped over. "And I'll bring you some snacks while you work!"

Max smiled. "Thanks, everyone. I feel so much better now!"

Professor ProjectManager clapped his wings. "That's teamwork in action! By supporting Max, you've shown how helpful small acts can fix big worries."

Roles in Action: Badges & Huddles

- **Team Badges:** Each friend decorates and wears a badge (Organizer, Helper, Checker, Reporter) to remember their job.
- **Daily Huddle (5 minutes):** "Yesterday I… / Today I… / I'm stuck on… / I need help with…" — a quick check to spot problems early.
- **Active Listening Game:** Repeat what someone said in your own words — practice super-listening!

These small routines keep everyone aligned and calm.

Feedback Stars & Inclusion

At the end of a meeting, give each other **one star** (a praise) and **one small suggestion**. Rotate who gives feedback so everyone learns to give and receive it kindly.

Ask: "Did every voice get heard today?" If someone seems shy, invite them gently — maybe they'll share with a thumbs-up or a drawing.

Reflection Time

Professor ProjectManager asked:

- "How did working together make the hard tasks easier?"
- "What did you learn about your teammates?"
- "How can we help someone who seems stuck tomorrow?"

Bella smiled. "When we helped each other, no one felt stressed or alone."

Max nodded. "And being helpful is a kind of leadership."

Key Takeaway for Kids

True teamwork means using your strengths, helping others, and running small routines (badges, huddles, feedback) so the team keeps moving forward together.

Final Inspiration:

"Real teams shine when everyone helps — and a little kindness makes big work easier."

(**Quick note:** *Leadership ideas are explored in more depth in* Chapter 16: Leadership & *Stewardship — see that chapter for leader checklists and stewardship tips.*)

Section 3:

Managing Uncertainty & Problem-Solving

Learn to try small, fix fast, and solve problems together — run mini-tests and use the Peace Plan. Spot risks, make backup plans, and bounce back stronger — turn surprises into superpowers.

Chapter 11

Try It Small First: Prototyping & Testing

The festival was getting closer, and the friends were buzzing with excitement. Professor ProjectManager gathered them once again.

"Now that you've set your goals and practiced working as a team, it's time to test your ideas. This is called **prototyping**—trying something small first to see what works, fix what doesn't, and make it better before the big day."

Mini-Festival

"Let's run a **mini-festival** today," said the professor.

"Each group will test one thing: a game, a song, or a snack stand. **Testing helps us learn and makes the real festival even better!**"

- Timmy set up a ring toss game.

- Bella hopped on stage to try a short skit.

- Max opened a mini snack stand with nuts and berries.

- Lily fluttered around, checking signs and decorations.

The clearing came alive with tiny festival fun.

Test Cards

When the test ended, the professor gave each friend a **Test Card** with three boxes:

- **Try** – What did you test?

- **Notice** – What happened?

- **Tweak** – What could you change?

Max filled his out:

- Try: "Nut snack stand."

- Notice: "The line was too long."

- Tweak: "Add a second basket for faster service."

The professor smiled. "Try **telling** in your own words what happened—that shows you really understand what worked and what didn't."

Tester Guests

To make it more fun, the professor invited nearby forest friends as **tester guests**.

"Ask your testers three simple questions," he reminded them:

1. "What did you like?"
2. "What was tricky?"
3. "What would make it better?"

The guests happily played, nibbled, and sang along—then gave honest answers.

One guest said, "The hoops were hard to toss over." Timmy realized his ring toss needed bigger hoops. Bella learned her skit needed shorter lines.

Tweak Session

The friends huddled together. "Let's each fix one thing together to make our mini-festival better," said Timmy.

- He made bigger hoops for the ring toss.
- Bella cut her skit lines in half.
- Max added another snack basket.
- Lily brightened her signs with bold colors.

The friends worked together to fix one thing each, making their mini-festival better.

"Sometimes small fixes make the biggest difference," the professor encouraged.

Quality Stamp

When each fix was tested again, the professor stamped a big green **QUALITY APPROVED** mark on their boards.

"The green stamp means **'Quality Approved'**—a sign your hard work is paying off!" he said proudly.

The friends cheered and danced as their festival test grew stronger and stronger.

Reflection Time — What We Learned

As the moon rose over the clearing, Professor Projecko asked with a smile:

- "What did testing help you discover today?"
- "How did small changes make a big difference?"
- "Why is it smart to test before the real event?"

Bella laughed. "My skit was funnier once I made it shorter!"

Timmy nodded. "And bigger hoops made my game easier and more fun."

The professor beamed. "That's the power of testing—try, notice, tweak, and improve!"

Key Takeaway for Kids

Testing your ideas in small ways helps you learn faster, fix problems early, and make your final project shine.

Final Inspiration

"Big success starts small—test it, tweak it, and make it great!"

Chapter 12

Conflict Resolution & Problem-Solving

The Great Forest Festival was getting closer, and the friends were working harder each day. But sometimes, even the best teams run into problems.

One morning, Timmy and Bella both wanted to decorate the snack stand.

"I picked the shiny leaves first!" said Bella, crossing her arms firmly.

"But I already planned the pattern in my notebook," Timmy argued.

Timmy and Bella felt upset until Professor ProjectManager arrived quietly with calm eyes.

"Every project has bumps in the road," he said kindly. "Today, I'll show you the **Peace Plan**—a way to solve problems together."

Owl Steps: The Peace Plan

The professor wrote five simple steps on a chalkboard made from bark:

Pause – Stop and take a breath.

Listen – Hear what your friend is saying.

Options – Think of different ideas together.

Pick – Choose the idea that works best for everyone.

Check-back – Later, see if it's still working.

"Let's try," said the professor gently.

Timmy and Bella paused. Then they listened as each shared their idea. Together, they came up with an option: Timmy would design the top row, Bella the bottom row. They picked that solution and promised to check back tomorrow.

Feelings Meter

To help, the professor showed a big **Feelings Meter** with happy, calm, unsure, upset, and angry faces.

"It helps you understand your feelings and calm down," he explained. "Remember, emotions can change — and that's okay. Feelings are important, but decisions should be made using facts and what you know!"

Bella pointed to "upset" at the start but moved her finger to "happy" at the end.

Timmy nodded, feeling calm again.

Turn-Talker Tool

Next, the professor handed them a silly plush acorn.

"Whoever holds this is the only one talking, so everyone has a chance to be heard. Everyone else listens carefully like a super-listener—someone who pays full attention without interrupting."

They laughed, but it worked—no interruptions, just listening and nodding.

Resolution Roleplay

"Let's practice!" said the professor. The friends acted out little skits:

- Who gets the last marker?
- Two friends want the same job.
- A game breaks—who fixes it first?

"Role-playing helps you understand how others feel," the professor explained.

After each roleplay, always ask: *What could we do differently next time?* **This helps us learn and grow.**

Afterward, they swapped parts to see things from another perspective.

"It feels different when you stand in your friend's shoes," said Lily.

Inclusion Effect

The professor reminded them, "When we solve conflicts kindly, everyone feels included."

Max added, "A kind smile helps everyone feel safe and welcome."

Team Signature

Finally, the professor held up a big leaf scroll: **The Peace Plan Promise**.

Each friend signed or drew a symbol to show their promise. They made a promise to follow the Peace Plan together—then celebrated with a funny peace dance.

Reflection Time — What We Learned

As the sun set over the forest, Professor Projecko asked gently:

- "How did the Peace Plan help us solve problems today?"
- "What happened when we paused and listened?"
- "Why does kindness make teamwork stronger?"

Timmy smiled. "When we listened, we found a solution that worked for both of us."

Bella nodded. "And it felt good to stay friends instead of arguing."

The professor twinkled. "That's real problem-solving—calm minds and caring hearts."

Key Takeaway for Kids

Conflicts happen, but with calm steps—pause, listen, explore options, pick, and check back—you can solve problems and stay friends.

Final Inspiration

"Peaceful problem-solvers make the best project managers!"

Chapter 13

Adaptability, Resilience, and Risk Mediation

The Great Forest Festival was almost here, but last-minute challenges tested the friends like never before.

The fireflies, responsible for providing evening lighting, couldn't gather due to unexpected rain. The squirrel teacher for the sustainable living workshop was delayed by the same storm. And an influx of participants for the craft competition created a shortage of materials.

The team gathered under the Golden Canopy, feeling overwhelmed.

"Everything is falling apart!" exclaimed Bella the Bunny.

Professor ProjectManager landed softly, his feathers glistening with raindrops. "Challenges like these are part of every project. What matters is how you respond. Let's talk about **Risk Mediation**, **Adaptability**, and **Resilience**."

Risk Mediation: Planning for the Unexpected

Professor ProjectManager spread out a fresh scroll. "Risk Mediation means identifying potential problems before they happen and taking steps to reduce their impact. Let's break it down:

1. **Identify Risks** – What could go wrong? For example, bad weather, supply shortages, or delays.

2. **Assess Risks** – How likely are they to happen, and how big of a problem would they cause?

3. **Plan Responses** – What can you do to prevent or reduce the impact of these risks?"

Timmy nodded. "So, if we'd thought about bad weather earlier, we could've prepared extra supplies or a backup plan."

"Exactly," said the professor. "Risk Mediation helps you stay ahead of challenges."

Adapting to Challenges

"To handle the challenges we face now, let's adapt," the professor continued.

- **Lighting Issue**: Max suggested using leftover materials to create temporary lanterns. Bella and Lily worked quickly to assemble them, ensuring the evening events could continue.

- **Workshop Delay**: The friends rearranged the schedule, offering an impromptu crafting session for the waiting audience while the squirrel teacher made their way.

- **Craft Competition**: Bella repurposed some decorations to provide additional supplies, ensuring every participant had what they needed.

Professor ProjectManager smiled. "Adaptability is about staying flexible and finding creative solutions in the moment."

Building Resilience

"Resilience," the professor explained, "means bouncing back stronger after setbacks. It's about learning from challenges and being better prepared next time."

Bella twitched her ears. "So, every problem teaches us something?"

"Exactly," said the professor. "For example, now you know the importance of backup plans for weather, extra supplies for workshops, and flexible scheduling. Resilience is what helps you turn challenges into opportunities for growth."

Why These Skills Matter

After solving the immediate challenges, the professor gathered the friends.

"Risk Mediation, Adaptability, and Resilience are essential because:

1. **They keep your project on track** – By preparing for risks and adapting to challenges.

2. **They foster creativity** – Flexible thinking leads to innovative solutions.

3. **They build confidence** – Learning from setbacks makes you stronger for the future."

Timmy nodded. "It's like a turtle's shell. It protects us from trouble, but we grow stronger every time we face a new challenge."

"Well said, Timmy," the professor replied with a smile.

Real-Life Resilience

"To make it clearer," the professor added, "imagine planning a school fair. If a guest speaker cancels at the last minute, you might adapt by inviting another speaker or shifting the schedule. If it rains, you move the fair indoors. These are the kinds of quick, creative decisions that resilience allows you to make."

The Festival Overcomes

With their newfound adaptability and resilience, the friends overcame every obstacle. Lanterns lit up the festival, workshops buzzed with energy, and every craft competition participant left smiling.

"This turned out better than I imagined!" said Max.

"And we wouldn't have managed it without staying flexible and bouncing back," added Lily.

Professor ProjectManager's eyes twinkled. "Remember, great projects succeed not because they're free of challenges, but because they adapt to them. You've shown incredible resilience and teamwork."

Reflection Time — What We Learned

As the rain cleared and stars peeked through the clouds, Professor Projecko asked kindly:

- "How did we handle the surprises that came our way today?"
- "What helped us stay calm and keep the festival on track?"
- "What can we do next time to be even more prepared?"

Bella smiled. "We didn't give up—we just found new ways to fix things."

Timmy added, "Each problem taught us how to be stronger and smarter."

The professor nodded proudly. "That's true resilience—adapting with courage and turning challenges into learning."

Key Takeaway for Kids

When things don't go as planned, stay calm, think creatively, and keep going. Every challenge makes you stronger and wiser.

Final Inspiration

"Strong teams don't avoid storms—they learn to dance in the rain!"

Section 4:

Responsibility, Sustainability & Leadership

Take responsibility for your team and your world: learn to use people, time, and stuff wisely while caring for the environment. Grow into leaders who inspire action and stewards who protect people and nature—so every project helps others and lasts well into the future.

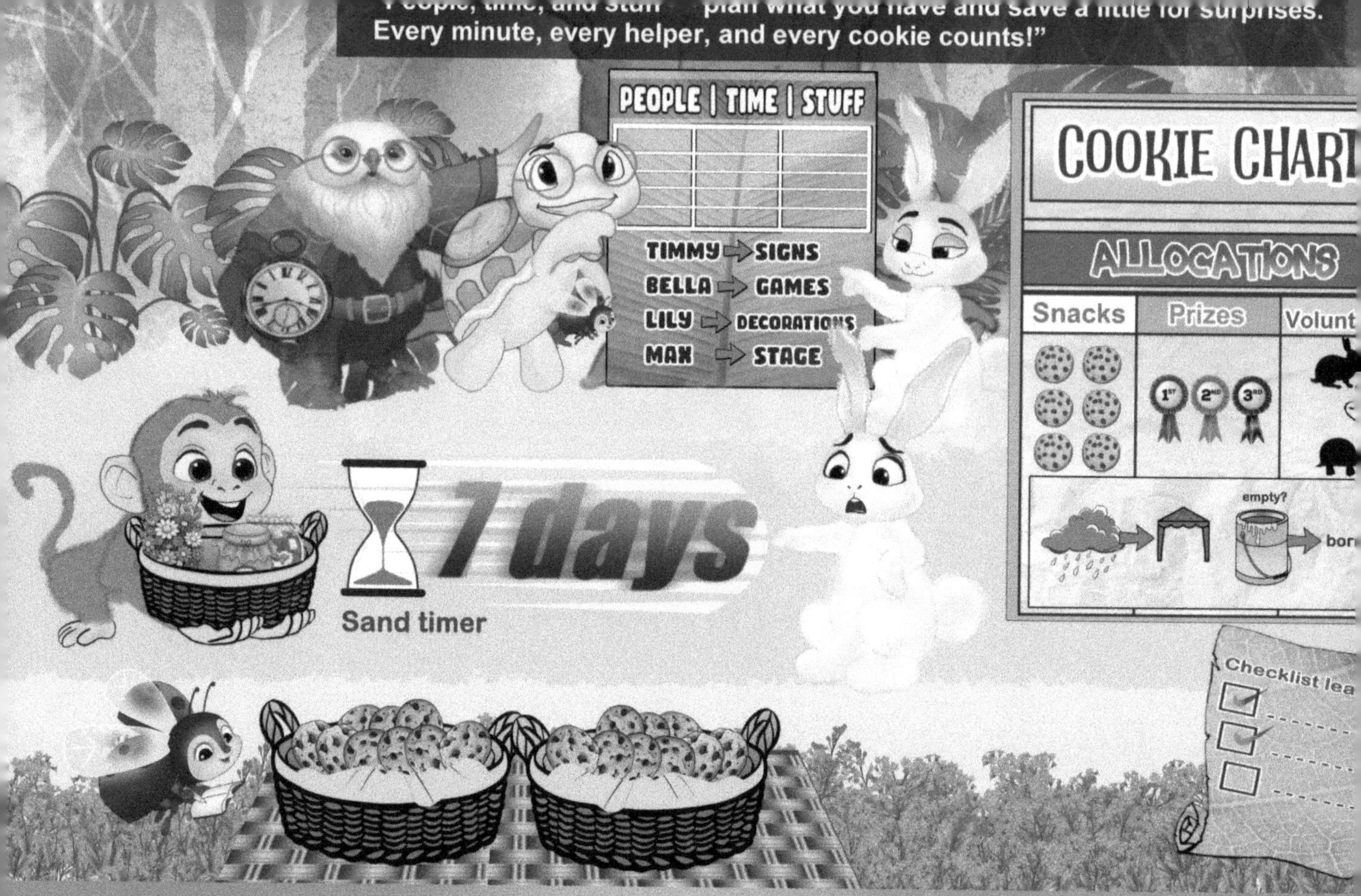

PEOPLE | TIME | STUFF

TIMMY ⇒ SIGNS
BELLA ⇒ GAMES
LILY ⇒ DECORATIONS
MAX ⇒ STAGE

7 days
Sand timer

COOKIE CHART

ALLOCATIONS

Snacks	Prizes	Volunt

1ST 2ND 3RD

empty?

bor

Checklist lea

Chapter 14

People, Time, and Stuff: Resources & Budgeting

The Great Forest Festival was only a week away, and excitement buzzed in the air. But Professor ProjectManager gathered the friends under the tall oak tree with a serious look.

"Before we invite more helpers or add new ideas," he said, "we need to think carefully about our **resources**—the people, the time, and the stuff we already have. Planning how to use them is called making a **budget**."

People Power

The professor pointed around the group.

"Timmy is steady and thoughtful, Bella is quick and helpful, Lily is creative, and Max is strong. These are your people resources. Each friend brings something important."

He added, "Sometimes we have lots of helpers, sometimes only a few. The key is to use everyone's strengths wisely."

Time Treasure

Professor held up a sand timer.

"Time is one of your most precious resources. You can't stretch it forever. We only have seven days until the festival. That means each task must fit into the time we have."

Bella crossed her arms. "So we can't spend all day just painting signs?"

"Right," said the professor. "If you spend too long on one job, there's no time left for others."

Stuff and Supplies

Next, the professor opened a big picnic basket. Inside were paints, brushes, wood, snacks, and flowers.

"These are your supplies. Sometimes you have plenty, sometimes only a little. The trick is to plan: how do we use what we have so nothing runs out before the big day?"

A Budgeting Story

The professor smiled and held up a plate of cookies.

"Let's say you have **20 cookies**. If you give **10** to the snack table, **5** for prizes, and **5** for the volunteers, that uses them all wisely. But if you spend **15** on decorations, you only have **5** left for snacks. See? That's why we make a budget—to plan our stuff so it lasts."

He added, "When we plan, we should ask: is this something we **need** or just something we **want**? Knowing the difference helps us make smart choices."

The friends giggled. Bella said, "Okay—no cookie banners!"

The Resource Chart

Professor drew three columns on a big leaf: **People | Time | Stuff.**

Together, the friends filled it in:

- People: Timmy (signs), Bella (games), Lily (decorations), Max (stage setup)
- Time: 7 days left, with one day for practice
- Stuff: 10 flowers, 5 baskets, 4 jars of paint, 20 cookies

Resource Shortage Scenario

Max frowned. "What if we need more paint than we have?"

"Good question," said the professor. "Here are some options:"

- **Borrow** from a neighbor 🎨
- **Substitute** another color 🖌
- **Ask for help** from a friend 🤝

"And if we use up too much too quickly," he added kindly, "that's okay. Mistakes help us learn to save better next time."

What Could Go Wrong?

The professor asked, "What might make us run out of time or supplies?"

The friends called out:

- "If it rains, the paint could wash away." → *Solution: cover stalls with tarps.*

- "If we forget the baskets, snacks won't be ready." → *Solution: make a checklist.*

- "If we spend too long decorating, the games won't be finished." → *Solution: set a timer for decorating.*

He nodded. "Spotting risks early helps us prepare. Planning ahead keeps problems smaller."

Saving, Sharing, and Giving

"Always save a bit of time and stuff for emergencies," the professor added.

"Share fairly. If one stall runs out of flowers, share from another. That's teamwork. And sometimes, giving a little treat to a visitor or helper makes the festival even more special!"

Reflection Time — What We Learned

At the end of the lesson, the professor asked:

- "Who are our helpers, and what are they best at?"

- "How much time do we really have?"

- "Did we use our stuff wisely? What will we do if we need more?"

- "Was this a need or just a want?"

- "What surprised us about planning resources?"

Bella smiled. "Next time, I'll share my paint before it runs out."

Timmy added, "And we'll save some cookies for emergencies."

Key Takeaway for Kids:

Every project needs people, time, and stuff. Planning how to use them is called a **budget**. Smart project managers know the difference between wants and needs, save a little for surprises, and share to help the whole project succeed.

Final Inspiration:

"Every minute, every helper, and every cookie counts—plan wisely, start early, and your project will shine!"

Chapter 15

Sustainability and
Environmental Stewardship
– Caring for Our World

As the Great Forest Festival wrapped up, the friends gathered for one final lesson under the Great Oak Tree. Professor ProjectManager stood before them, his feathers glowing in the soft lantern light.

"My dear friends," he began, "your festival has not only brought joy to the forest but has shown the importance of working together and growing as individuals. But there is one more lesson I want to share: the importance of **Sustainability** and **Environmental Stewardship**.

"Every project," he continued, "should not only benefit the present but also ensure a better future for those who come after us."

What Is Sustainability?

Professor ProjectManager drew a simple diagram on the ground:

- **Sustainability = Meeting our needs today + Preserving resources for tomorrow**

"Sustainability," he explained, "means meeting our needs today without using up everything the forest has to offer. It's about thinking long-term and making sure future festivals can enjoy the same beauty and abundance."

He paused thoughtfully. "Humans, too, face challenges like pollution and climate change. They depend on the oxygen we provide as we live in the forest. That makes us their stakeholders, just as they are ours. By protecting our home, we help not only ourselves but the wider world as well."

How the Festival Promoted Sustainability

The friends reflected on how they had incorporated sustainable practices into the festival:

- **Reusing Materials**: Lily the Ladybug buzzed proudly. "We used fallen branches and leaves to decorate instead of cutting fresh ones!"

- **Eco-Friendly Food Stalls**: Bella the Bunny added, "And the food stalls used biodegradable plates and cups to reduce waste."

- **Workshops on Sustainability**: Timmy the Tortoise nodded. "The workshops on sustainable living inspired everyone to think about how they can care for the forest."

The Power of Environmental Stewardship

Professor ProjectManager's eyes twinkled. "Stewardship is about caring for the world around us—just like caring for your team. Environmental Stewardship means:

1. **Protecting Resources** – Using only what you need and avoiding waste.

2. **Supporting Ecosystems** – Helping the forest and its creatures thrive.

3. **Teaching Others** – Sharing what you've learned so the whole community can grow."

Max the Monkey raised a hand. "Does that mean we should plant more trees for the next festival?"

"Exactly, Max!" said the professor. "Sustainability means giving back to the forest as much as we take. By planting trees, we ensure future festivals have shade, beauty, and plenty of materials."

Sustainability and ESG

Professor ProjectManager fluffed his feathers. "In the human world, they use something called ESG—Environment, Social, and Governance—to measure how responsibly projects are managed. Stakeholders, like investors, often evaluate whether a project supports the environment, benefits the community, and operates fairly.

"Here in our forest, reusing materials, involving the entire community, and working together with care would score high on ESG principles. Humans and animals alike benefit when we think sustainably."

Sustainability in Action

Inspired by the lesson, the friends brainstormed new ways to care for their forest:

- **Timmy** suggested creating a composting station for festival leftovers.

- **Bella** proposed organizing a "Forest Cleanup Day" after the festival to gather any waste and recycle what they could.

- **Max** volunteered to lead a tree-planting project with the younger animals.

- **Lily** offered to create a guidebook on sustainable practices to inspire others.

A Message for the Future

Professor ProjectManager's voice grew warm as he concluded. "When we care for the world around us, we create a legacy of growth and kindness. Sustainability is not just about preserving resources—it's about creating a better future for everyone. Let the lessons of this festival guide you in every project and every moment of your lives."

The friends looked at one another, their hearts full of determination.

Bella hopped excitedly. "We'll make the next festival even better—and even greener!"

Lily buzzed in agreement. "And we'll teach everyone how to care for the forest."

Timmy smiled slowly. "The forest has given us so much. It's time to give back."

Max swung joyfully from a branch. "Let's do it!"

The friends and the entire forest community began planning ways to care for their magical home, knowing their actions would make a difference for generations to come.

Reflection Time — What We Learned

As the lanterns dimmed and the forest glowed softly, Professor Projecko asked with a gentle smile:

- "How did we help protect our forest during the festival?"
- "What can we do next time to make it even more sustainable?"
- "Why is caring for our world a part of every great project?"

Lily buzzed proudly. "We reused and recycled instead of wasting!"

Timmy nodded. "And next time, we'll plant more trees for the future."

The professor twinkled. "That's true stewardship—caring for today while protecting tomorrow."

Key Takeaway for Kids

Sustainability means using resources wisely, giving back to nature, and ensuring our actions help both people and the planet thrive.

Final Inspiration

"Care for the world today—so it can keep caring for you tomorrow!"

Chapter 16

Leadership & Stewardship – Inspiring and Guiding the Team

The sun rose over the magical forest, signaling the final preparations for the Great Forest Festival. The festival grounds buzzed with activity—food stalls were being stocked, the bird choir rehearsed their final notes, and the craft competition area was decorated with colorful banners. But with so much going on, the team began to feel the weight of responsibility.

"I don't know if we'll get everything done in time," Timmy the Tortoise admitted, his voice slow but filled with worry.

Professor ProjectManager swooped down gracefully. "Timmy, this is the perfect moment to talk about Leadership and how it works hand-in-hand with Stewardship. Together, they guide the team and keep everyone cared for while staying focused on the goal."

What Is Leadership?

Professor ProjectManager perched on a low branch, addressing the team. "Leadership is about inspiring and guiding the team toward a common goal. A good leader doesn't just tell others what to do — they:

1. **Set an example** — work hard and stay positive.
2. **Motivate others** — encourage the team when challenges arise.
3. **Make decisions** — choose what's best for the project and the people."

Max the Monkey scratched his head. "But isn't a leader just the boss?"

"Not at all," said the professor. "Leaders serve the team by guiding it, and in doing so they help everyone do their best."

Leadership vs. Stewardship

Leadership focuses on direction and decisions: setting the goal, choosing the path, and making the call when the team needs direction.

Stewardship focuses on care: protecting the team's energy, coaching people, and making sure everyone has what they need. Great leaders do both — they guide the work and look after the people doing it.

Leading Through the Festival Tasks — Examples

- **Lighting Setup:** Timmy steadied the ladder for Bella — a leader noticing a need and stepping in.

- **Craft Competition:** Max encouraged nervous participants — leadership by example and cheer.

- **Food Stall Coordination:** Bella organized helpers to prevent a line — decisive action that eased stress.

These small actions show how leaders and stewards make the team stronger.

Leader Checklist

Use this quick card when you're leading a team:

Leader Checklist

- Set a clear daily goal for the team.

- Run a 1–2 minute huddle; remove one blocker.

- Notice one person who needs help; ask, "How can I support you?"

- Make one quick decision, then check back later.

- Celebrate at least one small win.

Stewardship Behaviors (doable habits)

- **Check in emotionally:** "How are you doing today?"

- **Share resources fairly:** make sure nobody runs out.

- **Teach, don't just tell:** show how to do a task.

- **Rotate hard jobs:** keep people from burning out.

These habits keep the team healthy and capable.

Real-Life Leadership & Stewardship

The professor shared a simple example: "For a school sports day, a leader organizes the events and decides timing. A steward checks on nervous teammates and helps with water bottles. Together they make the event fair and fun."

Lily buzzed thoughtfully. "So, being a good leader means putting the team first?"

"That's right," said the professor. "The best leaders guide with purpose and care."

The Festival Unites

As the friends worked together, their leadership and stewardship strengthened the team:

- Timmy's steady guidance kept everyone focused.
- Bella's energy inspired the team to keep going.
- Max's problem-solving ensured no task was left undone.
- Lily's organization brought everything together seamlessly.

On the day of the festival, the entire forest celebrated in harmony.

"You've done it!" Professor ProjectManager exclaimed proudly. "Through your leadership and stewardship, you've created something truly extraordinary. Remember, a great leader isn't just in charge — they stand beside the team and help everyone shine."

Reflection Time — What We Learned

Professor ProjectManager asked:

- "What one decision helped the team most today?"
- "Who needs extra support tomorrow?"
- "What small habit will you practice to be a better steward?"

Timmy added, "When we care for each other, the whole team succeeds."

Key Takeaway for Kids

True leadership means inspiring others through kindness, responsibility, and practical actions. Stewardship is caring for the people who do the work — do both, and the team will rise together.

Final Inspiration:

"Great leaders don't stand above the team — they stand beside it, guiding with heart and purpose."

Section 5:

Delivering, Reflecting, and Celebrating Success

Bring your project across the finish line, reflect on the journey, and celebrate the team's growth and success. Learn how to turn experience into improvements — and build a lasting legacy.

Chapter 17

Execution and Celebration – Delivering with Quality

The day of the Great Forest Festival had arrived. The sun shone brightly over the magical forest, and the friends stood proudly at the festival grounds, ready to see their hard work come to life. Everything they had planned, adjusted, and prepared was about to come together.

Professor ProjectManager joined them under the Golden Canopy for a final word of encouragement. "Today is the culmination of your efforts," he said with a twinkle in his eye. "**Execution** is where your plans turn into reality, and delivering with quality is what makes your project truly extraordinary."

What Is Execution?

"Execution," the professor explained, "is the act of carrying out your plans. It's when ideas become actions and results. Even the best plans mean nothing if they aren't executed well."

Max the Monkey scratched his head. "But what if something doesn't go as planned?"

"That's where your adaptability comes in," said the professor. "Execution is not about everything being perfect. It's about focusing on doing your best with what you have, solving problems as they arise, and delivering with excellence."

Quality in Execution

Professor ProjectManager then gestured to the festival grounds. "Delivering with quality means paying attention to detail and making sure every part of the project is the best it can be. Quality management is what ensures that all your hard work shines through. It includes:

1. **Consistency** – Making sure everything meets the same high standards.

2. **Attention to Detail** – Double-checking to ensure nothing is missed.

3. **Pride in Your Work** – Putting your heart into every task.

Quality Management — How we make it great (Kid Steps)

1. **Agree what "good" looks like.** Say one sentence: "Good = banner hangs straight and is readable."

2. **Check as you go.** After a friend finishes a task, another friend does a 30-second look: "Looks good?"

3. **Fix fast.** If something's wrong, make one small fix right away (no long delays).

4. **Quality Stamp.** When a task passes the check, give it a green ✓ or a small "QUALITY STAMP" sticker.

Bella the Bunny twitched her ears. "But isn't quality management just more planning?"

The professor chuckled. "Not exactly, Bella. Quality management happens during execution—it's about keeping your eyes open and your standards high as you bring the plan to life. And just as important as quality is **timely execution.**"

Timely Execution: A Critical Element

"As you execute your plans," the professor continued, "remember that timing matters just as much as quality. Even the best tasks lose their value if they're not completed on time. Imagine if the food stalls weren't ready when the festival began or if the bird choir missed their first song. Timing ensures that everything comes together seamlessly."

Timely Execution — Mini-rules to finish on time

1. **Mini-deadlines:** Break the day into a few target times. Example: "By 11:00 — stage ready; by 1:00 — food stalls open."

2. **Use a timer:** Set a 15–30 minute timer for focused work. When it rings, quick check-in.

3. **Do the critical path first:** If a task will delay many others, do it now. (Ask: "Will this slow down everyone else?")

4. **On-the-spot fixes only:** If something goes wrong and it can be fixed in 5 minutes, fix it now. If it needs longer, note it and move on.

Max tilted his head. "So, we need to focus on both doing our best and finishing on time?"

"Exactly," said the professor. "Managing your time wisely ensures that your efforts truly shine. It's a skill that will save you from regrets later—because sometimes, you only get one chance to deliver."

Applying Quality to the Festival

As the festival kicked off, the friends worked together to ensure every part of the event exceeded expectations:

- **Timmy the Tortoise** carefully checked the schedule, ensuring that every performance and workshop started on time. His steady attention to detail ensured the day flowed smoothly.

- **Bella the Bunny** hopped between the food stalls and craft competition, offering quick fixes and bursts of energy whenever a small issue arose.

- **Max the Monkey** solved last-minute technical problems with the bird choir's stage, ensuring the performances went off without a hitch.

- **Lily the Ladybug** buzzed through the festival, double-checking that every detail was perfect, from the decorations to the prizes for the craft competition.

Who watches for quality? (Quality Champions)

Give a quick role to one helper each hour — the **Quality Champion**. Their job for the hour: do two 30-second checks and give a "Quality Stamp" for anything that passes.

Quick Quality Routine (2 minutes)

1. **Look (30 sec):** Walk past the area.

2. **Ask (30 sec):** One question: "Is this safe and tidy?"

3. **Fix or Flag (30 sec):** Fix small things or put a flag on big items to return later.

4. **Stamp (30 sec):** Give a green ✓ when it's good.

The Power of Execution

As the day unfolded, Professor ProjectManager gathered the friends for a quiet moment. "You've done an incredible job executing your plans with excellence," he said. "Let me tell you something I once heard while flying over Silicon Valley: Some of the most successful people emphasize execution over endless planning. A simple idea executed flawlessly is far more valuable than a complex plan that's poorly carried out."

Timmy tilted his head. "So, the key is not just the plan—it's how we make it happen?"

"Exactly," said the professor. "Most projects fail not because of poor ideas but because they are poorly executed. What makes your festival special is not just the plans you made but the care and quality you've put into making those plans a reality."

The Festival's Success

As the festival continued, the friends marveled at how smoothly everything went:

- The bird choir's songs echoed beautifully through the forest, bringing smiles to everyone's faces.

- The craft competition showcased incredible creativity, and every young animal left feeling proud of their work.

- The food stalls buzzed with happy customers, with every treat prepared to perfection.

- The workshops inspired the forest community, leaving them with new skills and ideas to cherish.

Bella hopped excitedly. "We did it! The festival is perfect!"

Timmy nodded. "It's all because we worked together and paid attention to every detail."

Max grinned. "And did you notice? All the stakeholders seem to be here! The honey suppliers were at the food stalls, chatting with the bees, and even the squirrel workshop leaders looked so proud of their birdhouse displays."

Lily buzzed with excitement. "And the village leaders are here too! I saw Chief Acorn talking to the owl council near the craft competition. They looked so impressed!"

Professor ProjectManager's golden eyes shone with pride. "Indeed, my friends. Execution is where dreams become reality. And by delivering with quality, you've created something truly unforgettable—an event the entire community, including its leaders, will remember for years to come."

Real-Life Lessons on Execution

To help them understand further, the professor shared an example:

"Imagine a school play. Even with the best script, costumes, and stage design, the play will only succeed if everyone performs their role with care and attention. Execution is about making sure every actor knows their lines, every prop is in place, and every detail comes together to create a magical experience for the audience."

Max grinned. "So, execution is about bringing the plan to life with everything we've got?"

"Exactly," said the professor. "Execution with quality is what separates good projects from great ones."

A Celebration of Success

As the festival drew to a close, the forest gathered under the stars to celebrate. The friends felt a deep sense of accomplishment, knowing they had not only planned but executed their vision with excellence.

"We couldn't have done it without each other," Lily said, her wings glowing softly in the lantern light.

"And we wouldn't have succeeded without focusing on quality," added Bella.

Professor ProjectManager raised his wings. "Today, you've shown that great execution requires teamwork, adaptability, and attention to detail. Remember this lesson: No matter how big or small the project, delivering with quality makes all the difference."

The forest erupted into applause, and the friends beamed with pride, knowing they had created something extraordinary together.

Reflection Time — What We Learned

As the stars twinkled above the festival grounds, Professor Projecko gathered the friends for one final reflection:

- "What helped our plans turn into reality today?"
- "How did paying attention to quality make a difference?"
- "Why is finishing on time as important as doing your best?"

Bella beamed. "Every little fix and check made the festival shine brighter."

Timmy nodded. "And working carefully kept everything running smoothly."

The professor smiled proudly. "That's the magic of great execution—turning effort into excellence and plans into memories."

Key Takeaway for Kids

Execution means bringing your plans to life with care, teamwork, and pride. Quality and timing turn good ideas into something truly great.

Final Inspiration

"Dream it, plan it, do it—with care and quality that makes it shine!"

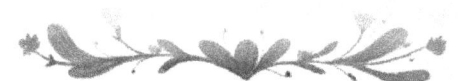

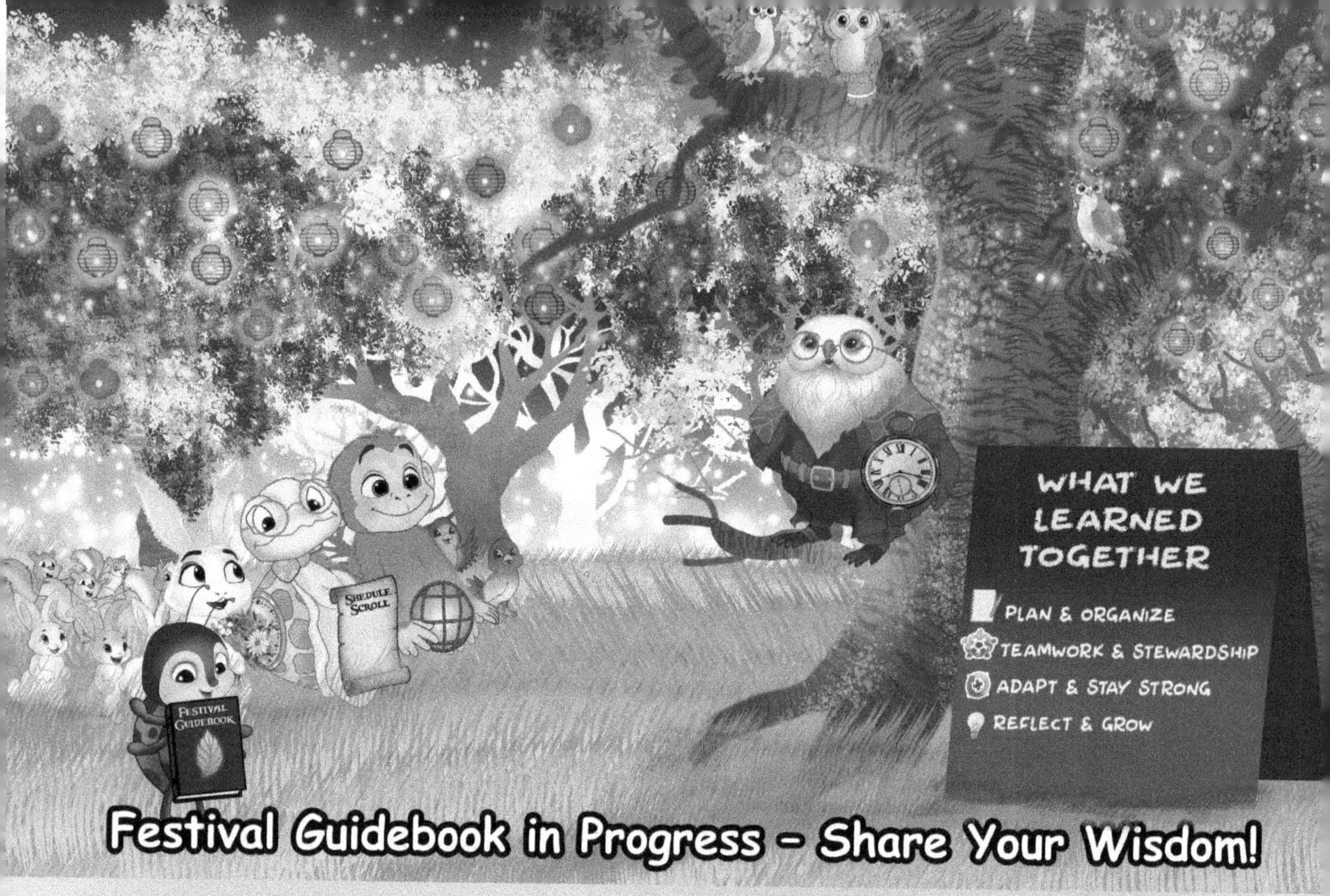
WHAT WE LEARNED TOGETHER
PLAN & ORGANIZE
TEAMWORK & STEWARDSHIP
ADAPT & STAY STRONG
REFLECT & GROW
FESTIVAL GUIDEBOOK
Festival Guidebook in Progress - Share Your Wisdom!

Chapter 18

Reflecting on the Journey – What We Learned

The stars twinkled above the magical forest as the festival came to an end. Lanterns cast a warm glow over the clearing, and the air was filled with the laughter of animals reminiscing about the day. The friends gathered near the Great Oak Tree, their hearts full from the festival's success, while other forest animals joined them to celebrate and reflect.

Professor ProjectManager perched on a low branch, his golden eyes shining with pride. "My dear friends," he said, "what a remarkable journey this has been. You've not only organized an incredible event but grown as individuals and as a team. Now is the perfect time to reflect on what we've learned."

The Power of Collective Growth

The professor invited Timmy, Bella, Max, and Lily to share their thoughts.

Timmy the Tortoise spoke first, his voice steady and thoughtful. "I've learned that even when things feel overwhelming, taking small, steady steps makes the impossible manageable. Planning and staying calm helped me keep us on track."

Bella the Bunny hopped up and twitched her ears. "And I've realized that energy and enthusiasm are powerful, but they need to be guided by teamwork. Working with everyone showed me how much more we can accomplish together than on our own."

Max the Monkey swung from a low branch and landed gracefully. "For me, the biggest lesson was about adaptability. When things didn't go as planned, we found creative solutions and turned challenges into opportunities."

Lily the Ladybug buzzed gently. "I've learned the importance of organization and attention to detail. Keeping track of everything ensured we didn't forget even the smallest tasks. But most importantly, I've learned that supporting each other makes the journey worthwhile."

As each friend shared their insights, the forest friends nodded in agreement. The squirrel workshop leader stood up, holding a small wooden birdhouse. "The teamwork we saw inspired us. We didn't just teach others to build—we learned the importance of building something together."

The owl council hooted in unison. "This festival has strengthened our entire community. Your growth has become our growth."

Embracing Challenges as Opportunities

Professor ProjectManager smiled. "This journey has taught us that challenges are not obstacles but opportunities. Every problem you faced led to innovation and growth.

- When the fireflies couldn't provide lighting, you created lanterns, showing resourcefulness.

- When the craft competition ran out of materials, Bella repurposed decorations to ensure everyone could participate.

- And when schedules needed adjusting, Timmy's calm approach kept everything on track.

Even beyond the festival, we saw the forest adapt. The beavers rebuilt their dam to prevent flooding, inspired by the teamwork they witnessed. The squirrels worked together to solve their acorn shortage, using lessons from the workshops."

Bella's ears twitched. "So, every problem made us stronger?"

"Exactly," said the professor. "Challenges foster resilience and innovation. They teach us to grow."

The Ongoing Nature of Learning and Stewardship

Professor ProjectManager continued, "Our journey doesn't end here. The lessons you've learned will guide you in future projects and adventures. But why not preserve these lessons for others?"

Lily's wings fluttered. "What if we create a wisdom journal—a guide to everything we've learned?"

Growth & Wisdom Journal

Keep a tiny journal to remember what worked and make future projects even better. Try filling out one page each project day.

Date: _____

Project: _____

1. **What went well today? (Win)** _____

2. **What surprised us?** _____

3. **What didn't go as planned? (Oops)** _____

4. **One thing we'll change next time:** _____

5. **Who helped and how?** _____

6. **My proud moment (draw or write):** _____

Reflection Prompts (for group time)

- "If we could do this part again, what would we try differently?"

- "Who helped the most today and why?"

- "Did we save enough for emergencies?" *(ties to budgeting)*

Teacher / Parent Tip:

Keep a decorated box for finished journal pages and let a different child be the **Keeper** each meeting. The Keeper reads a favorite entry at the end of the project to share what the team learned.

Max grinned. "We could call it the Festival Guidebook! Future festivals will be even better because of what we've written down."

The professor nodded. "A wonderful idea. By sharing your knowledge, you're practicing stewardship—not just caring for your team but ensuring the entire forest grows wiser."

The friends and forest animals worked together to compile their learnings, from planning and teamwork to adaptability and execution. As they wrote, they realized the journey of growth never truly ends—it continues with every project, every challenge, and every shared moment.

Looking Ahead

As the forest grew quiet, Professor ProjectManager gave his final words of wisdom. "Every journey has a beginning and an end, but the lessons you've learned here will last forever. Whether it's another festival, a new adventure, or helping others in their own projects, you now have the skills to make any vision a reality. Reflect on this journey, cherish these lessons, and carry them forward."

The friends looked at one another, their hearts full of gratitude.

Bella said, "Do you think we'll have another project like this?"

Professor ProjectManager smiled. "The world is full of possibilities, Bella. With what you've learned, there's no limit to what you can achieve. Just remember: every great success begins with a single step and grows with the care and effort you bring to it."

A Celebration of Success

The forest friends gathered under the stars to celebrate. The bird choir sang one last song, the lanterns flickered gently, and the forest glowed with community and joy.

"We did it together," Lily said softly.

"And we'll always have this journey to inspire us," added Max.

Professor ProjectManager spread his wings. "Reflect on this journey, my friends. Cherish the growth, and remember: every project is not just about the result but the transformation it brings. This is the legacy of the Great Forest Festival."

The forest erupted into applause, and the friends beamed with pride, knowing their journey was not just a project—it was a lifelong lesson in teamwork, leadership, and the power of growth.

Reflection Time — What We Learned

As the stars shimmered above the peaceful forest, Professor Projecko asked softly:

- "What lesson from our journey will you remember most?"
- "How did challenges help you grow stronger?"
- "What can we share to help others learn from our experience?"

Timmy smiled. "I learned that every step—big or small—matters when we work together."

Bella nodded. "And every mistake taught us something new."

The professor's golden eyes gleamed. "That's the heart of reflection—celebrating growth and using what you've learned to guide the future."

Key Takeaway for Kids

Every project teaches something valuable. Reflecting on what worked—and what didn't—helps you grow wiser, stronger, and ready for the next adventure.

Final Inspiration

"Look back with gratitude, learn with joy, and step forward with confidence—the best journeys never truly end!"

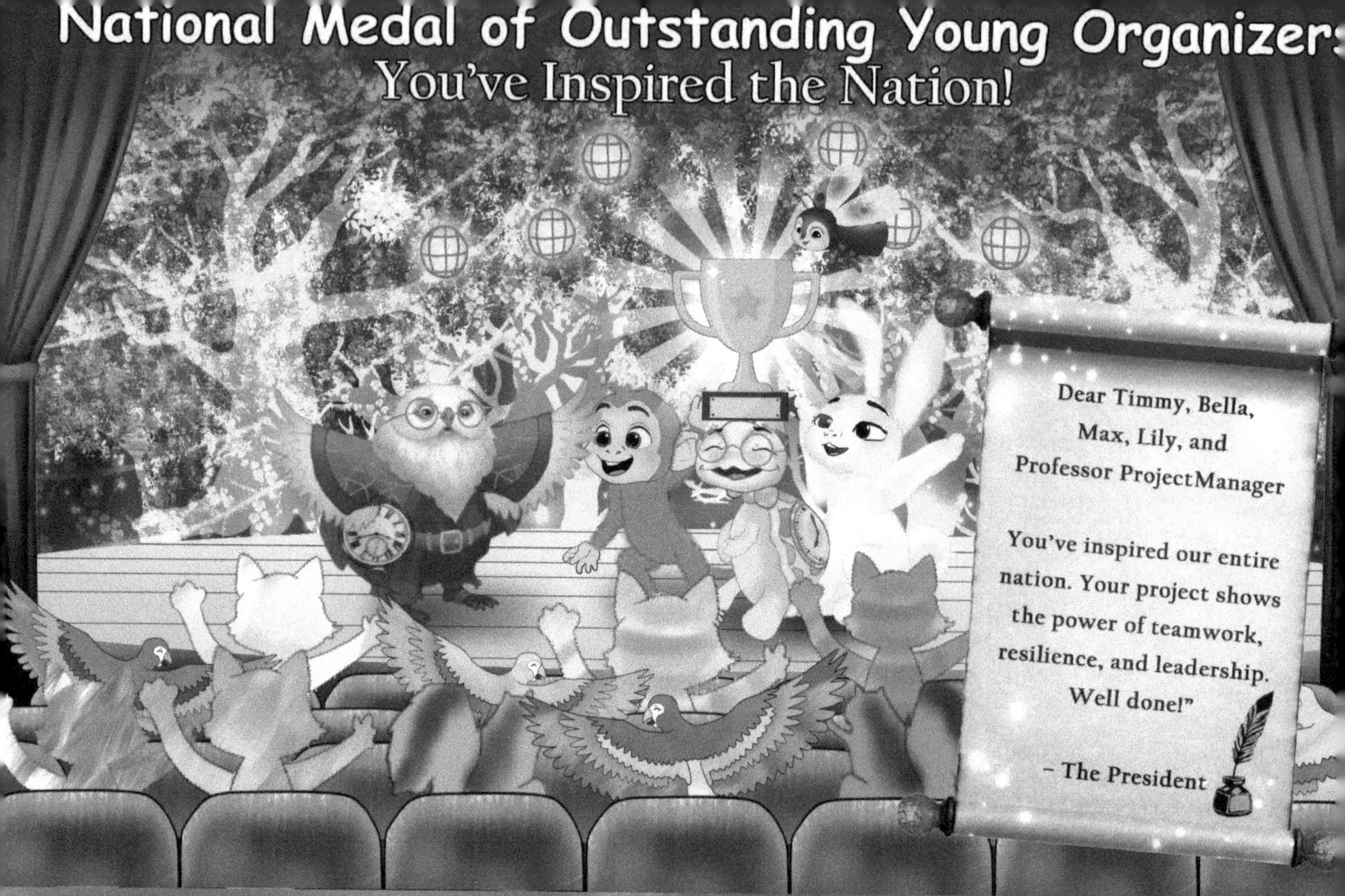

Dear Timmy, Bella, Max, Lily, and Professor ProjectManager

You've inspired our entire nation. Your project shows the power of teamwork, resilience, and leadership. Well done!"

– The President

Chapter 19

Epilogue: A Letter from the President

The Great Forest Festival had been a dazzling success. The decorations sparkled under the golden sunlight, the performers brought laughter and awe, and every creature from the magical forest had danced, eaten, and celebrated together. The festival had not just brought joy; it had shown what could be accomplished with teamwork, planning, and perseverance.

After the celebration, the friends reflected on their journey with Professor ProjectManager. They laughed at their initial missteps and marveled at how much they had grown. Each friend shared their biggest lesson, and the professor beamed with pride.

When the meeting ended, everyone parted ways, ready to take on new adventures with the skills they had learned. The professor flapped his wings and disappeared into the golden sky, leaving them to carry forward his wisdom.

An Unexpected Notice

A few days later, Timmy, Bella, Max, and Lily each received an official notice from the Great Village Authorities. It simply read:

"Your presence is requested at the Village Auditorium. Please report promptly."

The friends gathered at their usual meeting spot in the forest, puzzled and nervous.

"Do you think we did something wrong?" Timmy asked, his voice trembling slightly.

"But the City Mayor loved the festival," Bella replied, twitching her ears. "He even gave us an award!"

"Maybe we spent too many resources," Max suggested, scratching his head. "Did we use too many flowers? Too much honey?"

Lily buzzed softly. "Whatever it is, we need to show up. Ignoring the notice would only make things worse."

Reluctantly, the friends decided to go together. As they approached the grand auditorium, their nervous chatter faded into stunned silence.

A Standing Ovation

The auditorium was filled with dignitaries. Forest leaders, City Officials, and even villagers they didn't recognize were present. At the center of the room stood Professor ProjectManager, talking to the village authorities. When he spotted his young students, he waved them over.

"Come with me," the professor said warmly.

The moment they stepped into the room, the entire audience rose to their feet. Applause thundered through the auditorium as the friends walked in, their eyes wide with surprise.

"What…what is this?" Bella whispered.

Timmy's shell glistened under the light as he tried to shrink into it, overwhelmed by the attention.

At the front of the room, the Village Chief held up an envelope embossed with a golden seal.

"This," the Chief said, "is a letter from the President of the Land."

The room fell silent as the Chief opened the letter and began to read aloud:

The President's Letter

To Timmy the Tortoise, Bella the Bunny, Max the Monkey, Lily the Ladybug, and Professor ProjectManager:

I am honored to write this letter to commend you for your extraordinary accomplishment in organizing the Great Forest Festival. Completing a project is one of life's most rewarding challenges. It requires planning, teamwork, resilience, and leadership—qualities that are difficult to master even for the most experienced.

As someone who has completed many projects myself—and failed at many more—I know how tough it can be to see a vision through to the end. But you have proven that with dedication, collaboration, and the courage to learn from mistakes, even the most ambitious dreams can come true.

Your festival was not just a celebration of your forest; it was a shining example of what can be achieved when individuals come together to work toward a common goal. You have inspired not only your community but the entire nation.

I am proud to present you with the **National Medal for Outstanding Young Organizers** for your exceptional efforts. You have shown us all the true meaning of perseverance, creativity, and the power of working as a team.

Congratulations on your success, and may your journey of learning and growing never end.

With admiration and gratitude,

The President

Celebration and Pride

The audience erupted into applause once more. The friends stood in awe, their hearts swelling with pride.

"We… we did it," Max said, his usual cheeky grin now replaced with a genuine smile.

"Not just for ourselves," Lily added, "but for everyone in the forest."

Timmy nodded slowly. "All it took was one step at a time."

Bella bounced happily. "I can't wait to plan our next adventure!"

Professor ProjectManager stepped forward, his golden eyes twinkling. "Remember this moment," he said, "not just for the joy of success, but for the lessons you learned along the way. The real treasure of any project is how it helps you grow."

The Journey Continues

As the friends left the auditorium, they looked to the future with excitement and confidence. They knew that no matter what challenges lay ahead, they had the tools, the teamwork, and the determination to overcome them.

As they reached the forest clearing, Professor ProjectManager turned to them with a knowing smile. "Word of your success has traveled far," he said. "Your next project may be even more complex—but I have no doubt you'll rise to the challenge. The best adventures are yet to come."

Somewhere in the golden sky above, Professor ProjectManager soared, proud of his students and the seeds of success he had helped them plant.

Community Pledge
"We promise to share what we learned, plant one tree for next year, and help a friend plan their first project." — Signed: **Timmy, Bella, Max, Lily, and Professor ProjectManager**

NEXT STEPS — TRY YOUR OWN PROJECT

You did it with the Great Forest Festival — now try making something of your own! Use this simple starter to plan, play, and share.

1. **Pick a project idea:** (circle one) Party / Playground clean-up / Mini-show / Garden / Class project / Other: _____

2. **Our Goal:**

   We want to: _____

3. **Team & Roles** (choose 1 per person)

   Organizer: _____ Helper: _____ Checker: _____ Reporter: _____

4. **Three Milestone Flags** (mini-goals — write them)

   Start (Day 1): _____

   Middle (Halfway): _____

   Finish (Big Day): _____

5. **Done Checklist** (tick when done)

   ☐   Banner or sign made

   ☐   One practice or test run done

   ☐   Food or treats planned (if any)

   ☐   Place cleaned & safe for guests

   ☐   Everyone knows their job

6. **Quick Ritual — 1-minute color check (mini-deadline)**

   At each mini-deadline, everyone holds up a color: **Green = done, Yellow = almost, Red = need help.** If someone shows red, the team pauses for 60 seconds to decide one quick help step.

7. **Try it small first (mini-test)**

   Pick one thing to try today (game, snack, song). Test it on two friends and ask: "What worked? What was tricky? One idea to make it better?"

8. **Celebrate & Share**

Ask your teacher/parent for a 5-minute "show & tell" after the project. Take one photo or draw a picture to put in your **Growth & Wisdom Journal**. (See Chapter 18 for a journal page you can copy.)

Teacher / Parent Tip: Give a child the role of **Keeper** — they collect journal pages and read a favorite entry at the end of the project.

Reflection Time — What We Learned

As the friends walked home beneath the glowing moonlight, Professor Projecko asked calmly:

- "How did it feel to be recognized for your hard work?"
- "Which lesson will guide you in your next project?"
- "What promise will you make to yourself after this success?"

Timmy smiled. "I'll always remember that slow and steady truly wins the race."

Bella twitched her ears. "And that teamwork makes every dream possible."

Max nodded. "Even small ideas can grow big when you believe in them."

Lily buzzed gently. "And sharing what we learn keeps the magic alive for others."

The professor's golden eyes glimmered. "Then you've learned the greatest lesson of all—success is sweetest when it's shared."

Key Takeaway for Kids

Every ending is a new beginning. Celebrate your achievements, share your knowledge, and keep creating new adventures—because learning never stops.

Final Inspiration

"Carry your lessons forward, light the way for others, and remember—every project you complete plants the seed for the next great dream!"

Reflection & Closing

Reflect on what you built, celebrate what you learned, and carry the lessons into your next adventure.

Author's Note

Dear Reader,

Congratulations — you helped plan, fix, and launch something amazing. Project work teaches patience, creativity, and teamwork, and the little steps you take now will help you tackle bigger ideas later. Keep using the checklists, huddles, and journal pages in this book. Share what you learned with a friend, and remember: every new project is practice for success.

— Dr. Joy Chacko, PhD

Quick Reflection

- What was our biggest win?
- What surprised us today?
- One thing we'll change next time.
- Who helped most and how?

🌟 Bonus Resources:

Visit **SkillfulAdventures.com** for free toolkits, worksheets, and planners for kids, parents, and teachers.

Section 6:

Toolkit & Kid-Friendly Glossary

A tiny set of story-tested tools and simple words to help you plan, test, and finish real projects — checklists, quick huddles, and reflection pages that match the story. Use these pages to try ideas with your team; parents and teachers can copy or adapt them for school or home.

Chapter 20

Toolbox & Glossary: Pick. Try. Learn. Repeat

A set of simple, story-tested tools you'll actually use. Try 1–2 with your team; the rest are extras you can copy, print, or save for later.

How to use this chapter

Each printable appears in the chapter where it's used. Post copies at your huddle board or photocopy one for your group.

A — DONE CHECKLIST

DONE CHECKLIST — Great Forest Festival

Project: _____ Date: _____ Area: _____

Checkbox column:

☐ Banner hung

☐ Stage ready & safe

☐ Games set & checked

☐ Food/snack area ready

☐ Signs readable & placed

☐ Trash & recycling set up

☐ Supplies reserve

☐ Final tidy & welcome look

Quality Champion: _____ Stamp: _____

If any box is NO → quick fix & time estimate: _____

B — TIMELY EXECUTION CARD + HUDDLE SCRIPT

TIMELY EXECUTION CARD — Mini-Deadlines & Quick Huddle

Project / Day: _____

Circle one each mini-deadline: ◯   ●

Green = Done | Yellow = Almost | Red = Need help

Mini-deadlines:

1. By _____ (time): _____ (◯ /   / ●)

2. By _____ (time): _____ (◯ /   / ●)

3. By _____ (time): _____ (◯ /   / ●)

If RED → Who can help? _____ | Next short step (30–60 sec):
_____

Use a timer: Work 15–30 minutes → Quick check (1–2 min) → continue or swap

---

HUDDLE SCRIPT

Leader: "Green / Yellow / Red?" (Everyone shows color)

IF GREEN → "Great — next mini-deadline is _____."

IF YELLOW → "One quick fix — who will do it?" (Name)

IF RED → "Who can help now? 1, 2, 3 — go!"

End → Everyone claps once.

C — TEST CARD

TEST CARD — Try → Notice → Tweak

Tester name: _____ Activity: _____ Date: _____

TRY — What did we test? (draw or write)

_____

NOTICE — What happened? (what worked / what didn't)

_____

TWEAK — One small change to try next (short action)

_____

Ask testers:

1) What did you like?

2) What was tricky?

3) One idea to make it better.

D — GROWTH & WISDOM JOURNAL

GROWTH & WISDOM — Team Journal

Date: _____ Project: _____

1. **What went well today? (Win)**

   _____

2. **What surprised us?**

   _____

3. **What didn't go as planned? (Oops)**

   _____

4. **One thing we'll change next time:**

   _____

5. **Who helped and how?**

   _____

6. **My proud moment**

   _____

Teacher/Parent tip: Keep these pages in a "Keeper Box." Rotate the Keeper each meeting.

E — RESOURCE CHART (teacher/parent use)

RESOURCE CHART — People | Time | Stuff

People | Time (days/hours left) | Stuff (counts)

Row1: _____ | _____ | _____

Row2: _____ | _____ | _____

Row3: _____ | _____ | _____

Row4: _____ | _____ | _____

Was this a NEED or a WANT? (circle)

NEED / WANT — Notes: _____

Kid-Friendly Glossary

Planning — Making a simple map of what you want to do, the steps to get there, and who will help.

Scope — What is inside your project (what you will do) and what is outside (what you won't do right now).

Definition of Done (Done) — The clear checklist that tells you when a task or the whole project is finished.

Checklist — A list you tick when tasks are complete so nothing gets forgotten.

Milestone — A mini-goal that shows you've reached an important step on the way.

Priority — The most important thing to do first when you have limited time or helpers.

Critical Path — The sequence of tasks that must finish on time for the whole project to finish on time.

PERT (Program Evaluation Review Technique) — A simple way to guess how long a task might take by thinking about best, likely, and worst times.

Stakeholder — Anyone who cares about or is affected by the project (helpers, family, teachers, or neighbors).

Systems Thinking — Looking at the whole project to see how parts affect each other (how one change can ripple through everything).

Prototype (Try Small First) — A tiny test version of an idea so you can fix problems before the big day.

Execution — Doing the work from your plan and making sure things happen on time.

www.ingramcontent.com/pod-product-compliance
Lightning Source LLC
Chambersburg PA
CBHW041537120626
46551CB00019B/2736